HIBERNIAN
GREATS

Hibernian Greats

JIM JEFFREY

breedon **books**
PUBLISHING

First published in Great Britain in 2006 by

The Breedon Books Publishing Company Limited

Breedon House, 3 The Parker Centre, Derby, DE21 4SZ.

ISBN 1 85983 535 X

Printed and bound by Biddles Ltd, Hardwick Industrial Estate,
King's Lynn, Norfolk.

CONTENTS

DEDICATION

To Mum and Dad

Thanks

ACKNOWLEDGEMENTS

I would like to thank the players who appear in this book for their time in interviews. I am also grateful to them for allowing me to borrow items from their wonderful private albums. The remainder of the pictures are from my own collection. I am unable to trace the origins of every image, but I must acknowledge those sports photographers who braved all sorts of weather to capture such wonderful pictures down through the years.

Brian Johnson of Almondvale Programmes very generously allowed me to borrow his magnificent collection of Hibernian programmes, handbooks and many other items of interest. He was also a source of good advice and Hibs stories.

Finally, I would like to thank the staff at both the Mitchell Library in Glasgow and the National Library of Scotland in Edinburgh for their help in tracking down information and pointing me to some wonderful sources.

FOREWORD

I'm delighted to recommend Jim's book of Hibernian Greats. Having written the Hibs match programme for so many years and interviewed a host of Hibs heroes both past and present, he is ideally placed to put down on paper 10 wonderful careers.

Jim obviously had a dilemma in knowing who to leave out, and while he could have included all of the Famous Five team I think he was right to pick just a few and include other great Hibernian stars. Hibernian Football Club has long been associated with attractive football, and this book captures the essence of that excitement and style.

My father played in the great Famous Five side and was best man at Lawrie Reilly's wedding. Thus, as a boy I was brought up in the company of men like Eddie Turnbull, Gordon Smith and Willie Ormond. Their engaging stories of Hibs were fun to listen to, but beneath the surface I was gaining a valuable insight into the workings and togetherness of a great team.

With that background, it won't surprise anyone that I became something of a Hibs fan as a boy, and I watched and admired the likes of Joe Baker, Pat Stanton and John Blackley from the Easter Road stand. When I finally joined Hibs myself, I was extremely lucky to join an experienced squad of players. People like Arthur Duncan gave me a great grounding in the game, and in truth I learned so much playing alongside him. I could never quite work out Arthur's age, he was so incredibly fit, and when I see him today he hardly looks any heavier or slower. A great trainer, a wonderful player and a genuinely good man, Arthur epitomised all that was good in football.

Today my media work takes me back to all of my former clubs – Hibs, Rangers, Kilmarnock, Motherwell – and I know how much supporters like to recall the games, players and incidents of yesteryear. Jim's book will allow Hibs fans to do exactly that, and with 10 truly great performers to recall they are guaranteed to enjoy the read.

Craig Paterson

INTRODUCTION

Selecting 10 Hibernian greats was never going to be an easy task. Not, I hasten to add, because of any lack of choice, but rather in knowing who to leave out. My selection will please some, infuriate others and probably be challenged for some time to come.

My first dilemma was how to treat the Famous Five era. I could have quite easily named all five of that remarkable forward line and probably thrown in the likes of Combe, Govan, Shaw, Howie, Younger and Paterson for good measure. However, this would have made for an incredibly narrow focus and considerable repetition. Nevertheless, I couldn't pick just one player from this era, and in the end I settled on including Gordon Smith, Lawrie Reilly and Eddie Turnbull.

Smith merits inclusion as not only one of the most popular Hibernian players ever but as a Scottish legend. Winning Championship medals at three clubs (none of which were based in Glasgow) and playing with grace and elegance contributed to making him one of the best players ever produced north of the border. Lawrie Reilly, as Hibs most prolific marksman and an international hero, was similarly impossible to leave out. Finally, from that era Eddie Turnbull earned his place. Turnbull was a magnificent player for Hibs and then achieved similar status as a manager at the club.

Next up was Joe Baker. An explosive goalscorer, capped by England and then whisked off to Italy's top League, he was a wonderful talent. In the modern game, Baker (like Smith and Reilly) would have been worth millions.

From the 1960s I selected Pat Stanton and Neil Martin. Stanton was almost 'Mr. Hibs' at one stage. A quiet man off the field, he was a tremendously balanced performer on it. He emulated Eddie Turnbull in managing the club at one stage, but his greatest accolade is that, like Gordon Smith, he was admired for his style by fans of other clubs. Neil Martin had the briefest Hibernian career of the players in this book, but in a relatively short space of time he made a huge impact.

At the tail end of the 60s and into the 70s the talents of John Blackley and Arthur Duncan lit up Easter Road. Blackley was a calm and composed defender, while Duncan was a speed merchant on the wing. No player can better Duncan's Hibs appearance record, while Blackley came back to manage the club and was as popular as Stanton when he did so.

We can't live entirely in the past, and I wanted to give younger fans their place and recognise their heroes too. Franck Sauzée was an easy choice as everyone who saw him play or spoke to him was immediately won over. Charming, sophisticated and successful, he added a touch of glamour to Hibs in the late 1990s that seemed scarcely believable. He, like Joe Baker and Pat Stanton, would have pushed for a place in the Famous Five era.

Garry O'Connor departed for Russia in the course of writing this book. His was a different football era and to have expected him to spend his entire career at Easter Road, like a modern day Lawrie Reilly, would have been unrealistic, but in the early 21st century there were afternoons when he positively energised Easter Road with his all-action centre-forward displays.

Thus, we have 10 excellent players. Some defenders, some midfielders (wing-halves or inside-forwards in 'old money') and most forwards, but regardless of their position they all made a huge impact.

This book has been based around interviews I carried out with these players over many years, and here I want to put on record my sincere thanks for the time the players gave me. It still amazes me just how modest and approachable the Hibernian heroes are in the flesh.

Pat Stanton and Lawrie Reilly scaled the heights and yet constantly refer to the good players they were surrounded by and will never sing their own praises. They both have a lovely habit of treating the views of fans to be as valid as those of people who earn their living from football. Sadly, Gordon Smith and Joe Baker have both passed away in recent times, and they were cut from the same cloth. Gordon was a charming, gentle man who seemed at times bemused by the sheer warmth football fans felt for him. Joe Baker, who had a lovely sense of humour, I could call at any time, and he thoroughly enjoyed talking about football, past and present.

Bizarrely Franck Sauzée, despite being the only foreign player in this book, exhibited fractionally the greatest passion for Hibs. He seemed to be a man on a crusade at times, and it is a source of real regret that his spell managing Hibs didn't work out. Putting his managerial notes together on a Monday evening was a master class in drive and passion. He simply loved the supporters, the club and Scotland in general.

Finally, being editor of the Hibs programme during the Alex McLeish era at Hibernian was a wonderful experience. He brought a host of great players to the club and injected a sparkle about the place. It was Alex who introduced me to several of the players featured in this book, and he was as helpful a manager as a programme editor could ever wish for. A wonderful ambassador for the club and for Scottish football in general, it is to him I owe the biggest vote of thanks.

Jim Jeffrey
May 2006

GORDON SMITH

There are many who say that Gordon Smith is the most artistic footballer ever to have graced the Scottish game. Athletic, aware, purposeful, supremely gifted... the accolades simply rolled in for this great winger. But to categorise him as merely a winger is to do him a great disservice.

Smith played senior football for a staggering 23 years! He won three Championship medals with Hibernian, another with Hearts and yet another with Dundee. Five Scottish Championship medals... and not one of them won while with the Old Firm. No player before or since has achieved that, nor is it likely that any ever will.

The son of Montrose grocer Robert Smith, Gordon was born in 1924. He was a highly-talented schoolboy footballer, being capped twice by Scotland at that level. As Smith himself noted:

'I was always football daft. My mother said I was kicking a ball about when I was three years old, imitating, no doubt, my two elder brothers. Maybe they had something to show me, for, by the time I was nine, I had played my first game for Southesk School. I played on the Saturday mornings and in the afternoons rushed down to Links Park to see my Montrose heroes.'

Smith had been a centre-forward as a schoolboy, but when he picked up his first Scottish schoolboy cap it was as an outside-right, and that was the position where he would make his senior reputation. He reckoned he was too small to lead the attack. How fortunate that his school – Montrose Academy – hadn't managed to convert him to rugby. By the time he was 16 years old he was playing with Dundee North End on a Saturday and working in an insurance office during the week.

As his reputation as a quality young player grew, he starred for a junior select XI against a combined Hibs-Hearts team in April 1941. The occasion was a match to mark the opening of Beechwood Park in Dundee. Smith, who had been with North End since November 1940, scored three times in that game, and Hearts very nearly signed him. Newspapers carried reports suggesting that he was a Hearts player, but it soon emerged that he had signed nothing and that Hearts actually wanted him to play in a trial game a few weeks later. While they dithered, Willie McCartney, the Hibs boss, made a very decisive move. Hearts may have presumed they had him signed, but McCartney arranged a meeting in Arbroath where he shrewdly pointed out that Hearts, in offering a trial, were stating that they had some doubts about his ability. Hibs, he emphasised, were keen to sign him there and then. McCartney must have been persuasive because Smith was a bit of a Hearts fans and keen to go to Tynecastle.

Ever the gentleman, Smith asked for time to think about the deal, and having talked it over with his father decided that he liked McCartney and liked the idea of joining Hibs. He travelled through to Edinburgh on an April Monday in 1941 to not only sign but make his debut that afternoon against Hearts. Smith would tell me later that his abiding memory was receiving a £10 note as a signing-on payment. 'Truth is, I felt incredibly rich having earned such a fee,' he confessed. Buoyed by his new riches, he scored a hat-trick as Hibs handed out a 5–3 defeat to their city rivals. It was the start of a wonderful relationship.

It would be wrong to ignore 'the team behind the team' at Easter Road in the immediate post-war era. Chairman Harry Swan and manager Willie McCartney forged a great relationship in the boardroom at Hibernian and the benefits filtered down in impressive fashion. It was surely their drive that laid the foundations for Hibs landing three Championships in a wonderful five-year period, and in signing Smith they completed perhaps their smartest piece of business.

Like many players of this era, Smith saw his early football career disrupted by the war. He featured regularly in the first team, but the competitions were 'unofficial' as the nation concentrated its efforts on

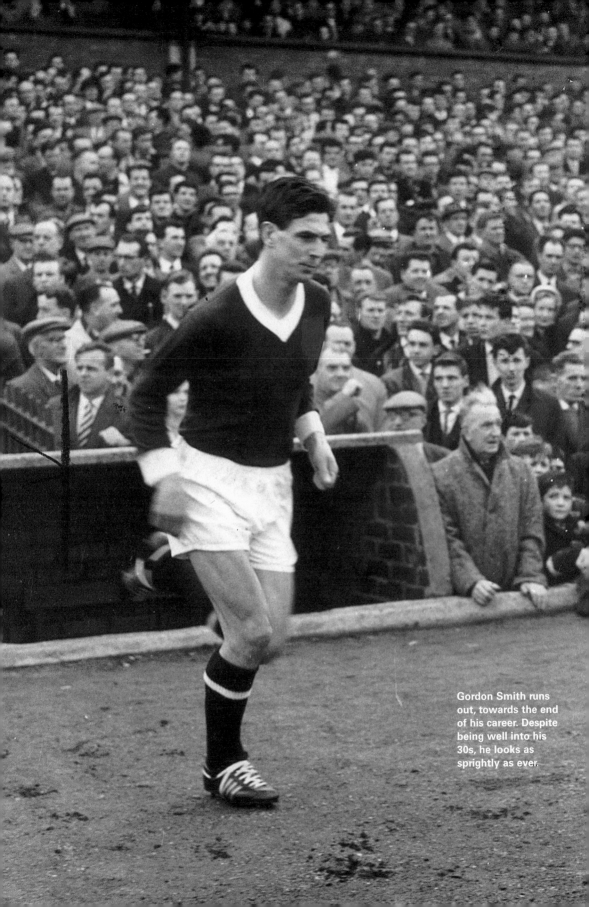

Gordon Smith runs out, towards the end of his career. Despite being well into his 30s, he looks as sprightly as ever.

THE SCOTSMAN, SATURDAY, MARCH 30, 1963

TWENTY-TWO YEARS ON

1949—It is no coincidence that Gordon Smith often plays before large crowds, as he will do at Dens Park this afternoon against Rangers. Here he is at his peak—and Hibs' too—scoring against Rangers at Ibrox, past Woodburn and Brown, the goalkeeper.

1943—A picture taken two years after joining Hibs.

1953—Ten years, nearly 300 goals and 500 appearances later.

1963—Training on the beach at North Berwick.

In 1963 *The Scotsman* carried a glowing tribute to Gordon Smith that covered his 20-plus years in the senior game.

World War Two. At this stage he was back to playing as a centre-forward, but when the Summer Cup came around he was moved to outside-right. He confessed that initially he was surprisingly uncomfortable in that position, especially with the responsibility of having to take corners and throw-ins. That first season saw Hibs win the Summer Cup, and although Smith didn't play in the Final he contributed mightily in the run up to it.

In September 1941 Smith played in the famous 8–1 League win over Rangers, scoring the last goal while running with his shin-guard in his hand. He told me a lovely story about that game many years later:

'After the match I would walk home or catch a bus. This was in the era before footballers were really famous and quite normal practice. I remember that after that game I walked out of the ground and round to the nearest bus stop. There a fan was reading his sports paper and said to me "It says here that Hibs beat the Rangers 8–1, what nonsense, it must be a mis-print." When an eight is poorly printed it can look like a zero, so I knew what he meant, but I was able to say "No, it isn't a mis-print it's right enough, it was 8–1. I know, I was there!"'

The war years foretold of the Hibs successes in the immediate post-war era. To the Summer Cup triumph of 1941 was added the Scottish Southern League Cup in 1944 and this time Smith did play. Unusually for modern readers, this match was decided on corner-kicks, as was the norm in the post-war era, well before the advent of penalty deciders.

When football returned to normality after the war, Hibs were quick out of the blocks. The very first game of the 1946–47 season saw Hibs entertain Queen of the South, and what a feast they provided after the famine of the war years. With a display of scintillating attacking football, Hibs hammered the luckless Dumfries side by a whopping 9–1. That set the tone for a season in which Hibs excelled, but unfortunately Rangers bettered them. When the final reckoning came, the two sides were separated by just two points. Galling for Hibs was the fact that, while they had taken three of the four points available against the Glasgow side, two defeats to Motherwell were probably crucial. It was a season full of promise but short on delivery. The Scottish Cup Final was lost to Aberdeen (despite Hibs being 'gifted' a goal in the opening minute), and Rangers won a pulsating League Cup semi-final 3–1 at Hampden Park.

The following season saw Hibs make no mistake and land the title. This time the battle with Rangers was reversed, and it was Hibernian who edged

Gordon featured in dozens of trade and cigarette cards during his career. These examples show him in the colours of Hibernian and Scotland.

home by two points. At one stage the Hibees won 10 matches in succession, and by the time they lost the final game of the season to Dundee at Dens Park it was academic as the title was already at Easter Road. However, joy was tinged with sadness as the man who made Hibs, manager Willie McCartney, died, having been taken unwell during a Scottish Cup tie at Albion Rovers. McCartney was desperate to guide Hibs to the League flag and had stated that it would be the happiest day of his life if Hibs could win their first title since 1903. Hugh Shaw took over running the team and guided Hibs to the Championship, but the loss of McCartney was keenly felt.

Smith's role in the Championship-winning side was immense. Not only was he the creator of a host of chances for his teammates, but he was top scorer too with 19 goals in his 29 appearances. The personal highlight must surely have been on 8 November when Third Lanark were dumped 8–0 and Smith scored five, and that heralded the start of a three-season spell in which the 5ft 9in player was top scorer each and every season. His finest performance was perhaps in the 1949–50 campaign when he scored a very impressive 25 goals in only 29 matches.

The Famous Five of Smith, Johnstone, Reilly, Turnbull and Ormond dominated this period, and Smith was voted Scotland's Player of the Year in 1951. Just how key they were to the success of Hibs in the era is demonstrated by the 1952–53 season, when Hibs scored 93 League goals and 'the Five' had no fewer than 85 of them. Smith, with his fleet-footed movement and telling crosses, was a class act on the right, while Ormond performed similar heroics on the left. Lawrie Reilly was the grateful recipient of many of Smith's wonderful crosses and hugely admired the graceful winger:

'Gordon was my boyhood hero, and I was lucky enough to get to play with him. He was the best player I have seen at Hibs, different class; he was the longest serving member of the Famous Five and led by example. We all loved him, and although he was quiet and not really in any group at Easter Road he was able to relate to everyone.'

I once asked Smith if he had a favourite triumph among the three title successes, and not surprisingly he found it hard to separate them:

'I think it is fair to say that we all took different pleasures from each of the three titles. I also remember the time we were pipped for another title on goal average. We had a wonderful side at Easter Road during that period.'

A non-smoker and tee-totaller, Smith was a thorough gentleman off the field. Ever the sportsman, he could absorb the punishment dished out by robust full-backs without complaint and was extremely popular among his fellow professionals. He was quite shrewd when it came to business too and soon had a grocer's shop in Willowbrea Road. He had four brothers and one sister, and the shop was often staffed by his siblings.

The press adored Smith and that adoration was enduring. My first seat in the Easter Road press box was beside the inimitable Edinburgh journalist John Gibson, and he was never slow to praise him, even chastising me when I once mistakenly compiled an all-time great Hibs XI and omitted him!

Following one famous win at St Mirren, the *Sunday Post* was moved to say:

'Other wingers might copy Gordon Smith and operate twenty to thirty yards infield. But could they trap the ball as deftly, elude the tackle and, with a perfect pass (long or short as occasion demanded), set the entire machinery of attack in motion?'

Both Newcastle United and Aston Villa offered £25,000 for Smith, but he was known at the time as the £40,000 player... a figure then deemed impossible to pay for a footballer. When Hibs ripped Tottenham apart in London, he became one of the most talked about footballers in England, but he steadfastly refused to contemplate a move south. Contented on the field, he was equally at ease with his life in the East of Scotland.

Hibs were pipped for the title in 1950 by a single point by Rangers. They had scored 86 goals compared to Rangers' 58, but, in losing both Edinburgh derby fixtures and bizarrely coming unstuck against little Third Lanark at home, the title slipped away. The Famous Five had done their bit; only seven players scored League goals for Hibs and the contribution of the two non-Famous Five players was just seven goals. Thus, Smith, Johnstone, Reilly, Turnbull and Ormond scored 79 of Hibs 86 League goals!

Season 1950–51 perhaps marked the high for this talented Hibs team. They won the title by a staggering 10 points over Rangers, and it would have been a domestic double but for a surprise League Cup Final defeat by Motherwell. In the League Hibs lost twice to Hearts but crushed Rangers 4–1 in April and Celtic 3–1 in the final match of the season. The win over Rangers caught the eye, and the *Evening Dispatch* noted:

'With Gordon Smith back in the side to inspire them, the Hibs established a two-goals lead by the interval, Johnstone and Reilly being the scorers. And to add to the discomfiture of Rangers, Gordon Smith himself scored two picture goals in the second half.'

It is difficult to exaggerate how regularly newspapers were brimming with their praise of Smith. The following extract from the *Sunday Express* was typical of the depth of feeling for him at this time:

'Hibs captain Gordon Smith is to me now and probably for the remainder of his career the greatest footballer in the land. For perfect body control and balance, for screening a ball from the tackle with his foot, for clicking it from one foot to the other, giving the tackler an extra yard to reach, for, well, I haven't got the space to ramble. But he leads his side with a style that is as sparkling as a mackerel in the moonlight.'

If Smith had one failing in his career it was that he seldom reproduced his Hibernian form when wearing the dark blue of Scotland. He made his debut for Scotland in an unofficial game against England in October 1944, yet he would win only 18 full international caps. He was unlucky that there was fierce competition for the right-wing position from Willie Waddell of Rangers and Jimmy Delaney of Celtic.

Smith captained Hibs in the early 1950s and was a popular choice when twice selected to lead Scotland in 1955. In the first of these games, against Austria in Vienna, he gave what was probably his best international performance, scoring the second goal as Scotland romped home 4–1. The team then travelled to Budapest, where they faced the mighty Hungarians. The captain gave Scotland the lead after 41 minutes, before the Hungarians imposed themselves to win by 3–1.

Smith's last international was in 1957, when Scotland lost 1–4 to Spain in a World Cup qualifier. Again, though, he had the satisfaction of scoring.

Poise and elegance
are captured in this
very early picture of
Gordon Smith at
Easter Road.

'I won 18 caps at full level and 10 Scottish League caps. There were some memorable games, and I played against England. Luckily I played with Lawrie Reilly a few times. Lawrie was a very, very good internationalist. If anything, he raised his game for Scotland matches whereas I don't think I really managed that.'

By the autumn of 1957 Smith was a legendary figure in Scottish football. He made his 500th appearance for Hibs against Queen of the South in the opening game of the season and then gave a virtuoso display in the League Cup at Morton. As Hibs romped home 6–0 at Cappielow Park, one scribe was completely won over by Smith:

'Smith turned in a sparkling display. One spectacular run in particular will be remembered. The winger trailed the ball from right to left of the field, beating five men in the process, to finish with a power drive that tested Cowan in the Morton goal to the full.'

On 15 September 1952 he had enjoyed a testimonial match against English champions Manchester United. This benefit game turned into one of the most sumptuous footballing occasions ever witnessed in Edinburgh.

'That was a marvellous game, and they had a good side at the time. Matt Busby helped organise that fixture as he had played with Hibs during the war.'

In a display of all-out attacking Hibs won 7–3, but the real winners were those lucky enough to be present. The match reporter for *The Scotsman* was clearly bowled over as he waxed lyrical in the following morning's paper:

'The match provided the finest football entertainment I have ever seen… in football artistry it far surpassed anything seen in Edinburgh, either that I have witnessed myself or heard of… if all games were like this all grounds would need to be Hampdens.'

Manchester United, for their part, at this time were extremely friendly with Hibs and had provided the opposition in September 1948 when Easter Road hosted a testimonial match for Willie McCartney. And Smith loved testimonial matches. By the time he turned out in Lawrie Reilly's benefit game in December 1958 he was a veteran but prepared to relax his then habit of not playing in Monday night games to honour his teammate. In that 9–3 win over an International Select, Gordon Smith scored goals number eight and nine.

While Smith was lithe and assured on his feet, he was not immune to injury, and twice he suffered broken legs. His teammates would later reveal that he often took to the field with his ankles swathed in bandages. It was injuries that convinced Hibs to release him in 1959, believing that he was a spent force. How wrong they were! Hearts snapped him up gleefully. He made his Hearts debut against Kilmarnock in an August League Cup tie, but an indication of his status had been seen in a reserve game a few days earlier, when over 10,000 turned up in the expectation of seeing the great Smith. Hearts benefitted greatly from his input and romped to the League Cup Final, where, with a delicious sense of irony, Hearts won the Cup. Smith, after 18 years of trying at Easter Road, had a major domestic Cup medal within months of arriving at Tynecastle.

It was to be a double-winning season for the Maroons as they raced to the League title. This, of course, brought entry to European competition, and, having been over the hurdles with Hibs, Smith's experience was relished. Thus, in two seasons at Tynecastle he won a Cup medal, a League Championship badge and played in Europe again.

In April 1961 Hearts granted Smith a free transfer. Once again he bounced back from this set-back with a major triumph. Dundee, who eagerly signed him, had never won the League Championship and indeed had been a mid-table side in the 1960–61 season. But with Gordon Smith in their ranks they were transformed. He missed only two League games and chipped in with seven goals, including one in a 3–1 win at Easter Road. It was a most unexpected Championship triumph for one of Scotland's provincial clubs.

Smith himself noted:

'I was very proud of that achievement to be quite honest. Dundee had a super team when I was there, and I really enjoyed playing up front with Alan Gilzean and Alan Cousin. I really felt that the Dundee team was on a par with the Hibs side I played in.'

The support he was able to give to blossoming young striker Alan Gilzean had been crucial (Gilzean scored 24 goals in only 29 matches), and Smith was still there the following season as Dundee entered the European Cup. He scored in both legs of the quarter-final against Anderlecht and had one in the famous 8–1 demolition of Cologne.

Amazingly, in season 1963–64 Gordon Smith was still playing top-flight football. He played in three League Cup ties and nine League matches before finally calling it a day. His last game in Scottish senior football was on New Year's Day 1964 at Dens Park against Aberdeen.

How did he manage to sustain himself at the top for 23 years?

'I was always fairly fit, although you could only do the normal training at the club as they didn't encourage you to do your own thing. I had some bad injuries in my career. One thing that interested me was the way broken legs were covered in the newspapers. The tibia is the shin bone and a few inches wide. If it breaks then playing on is impossible. However, the fibula was the smaller bone and it had happened that players played on with the injury. I remember you would go to the likes of Airdrie and they would pump the ball up until it was like a stone, then if it got wet it got even heavier. Also players wore toe-caps so all in all I think broken bones were more common and the game was certainly different in many ways.'

Many shrewd observers of the game reckon that Smith was the greatest Scot of them all. Bob Crampsey, the veteran football historian and writer, told me so several times, and Alastair Alexander, who commentated on hundreds of games for BBC Scotland, was of a like mind.

'Smith was the most complete Scottish player I ever saw. He was ahead of his time and a wonderful athlete and footballer. He looked after himself so well that he was able to enjoy a phenomenally lengthy career at the top level. It is the fact that he gained Championship medals at Hibs, Hearts and Dundee that makes him so special in my book.'

Gordon Smith was, above all else, a real gentleman. His hugely successful career never changed him from the shy, unassuming man, beloved of the Easter Road faithful but happiest at home in North Berwick. He would as happily speak about playing with his cat as his football career. It was Hibs' good fortune to have such a player in their ranks for such a lengthy period.

GORDON SMITH factfile

Born: Edinburgh, 25 May 1924
Position: Right-winger
Playing career: Hibernian, Hearts, Dundee

Hibs League career:

Season	Games	Goals
1946–47	23	7
1947–48	29	19
1948–49	29	15
1949–50	29	25
1950–51	25	10
1951–52	29	9
1952–53	28	13
1953–54	12	5
1954–55	28	9
1955–56	30	7
1956–57	17	3
1957–58	16	3
1958–59	15	1
Total	310	126

International caps:

One Scotland Schoolboy cap

One Scotland wartime international cap

Scottish League: 10 games

Scotland: 18 games (4 goals)

SMITH'S GOALSCORING RECORD

Smith was Hibernian's top scorer in the League in seasons 1947–48, 1948–49 and 1949–50.

The breakdown of his domestic goals is as follows:

15 – Motherwell, Queen of the South

13 – Third Lanark, St Mirren

12 – Aberdeen, Clyde

11 – Falkirk, Airdrie

 9 – Dundee, Raith Rovers

8 – Partick Thistle

7 – Rangers

6 – Stirling Albion

5 – Hearts, Celtic

4 – East Fife

3 – Morton

2 – Albion Rovers, Arbroath, Dunfermline Athletic, Kilmarnock, Queen's Park

1 – Ayr United, Dumbarton, Hamilton, Stenhousemuir

The above figures represent League, Scottish Cup and League Cup goals. Not included are goals scored in the European Cup, St Mungo Cup, Coronation Cup, East of Scotland Shield and Friendlies.

EDDIE TURNBULL

When Eddie Turnbull paraded his no-nonsense array of inside-forward talents at Easter Road in the 1940s and 1950s, he could hardly have been expected to return to the famous old ground and carve out a career as one of Scotland's clearest-thinking coaches. Yet he did. For all the 'power play' of his youth, he was clearly observing technique and talent in the Hibs engine room. By the time he was boss at Hibs in the 1970s he had gathered enough knowledge to create one of the finest post-war Scottish sides.

It is Turnbull's link with the Famous Five and Turnbull's Tornadoes that earns him a special place in the history of Hibernian. Some may say his finest moments were helping the club reach the European Cup semi-final in 1955 or winning three Championships. But others, with equal justification, would say that in creating the side of Brownlie, Stanton, Blackley, Edwards, O'Rourke, Gordon, Cropley and Duncan he gave back to Hibs fans their love of good football above all else.

A noted schoolboy player, Turnbull had served in the Merchant Navy in Portsmouth but was very much a central Scotland boy. He was from Carronshore, which in a footballing sense was rather appropriate as the area was famed for the Carron Company. A bulwark of the industrial revolution, it had made its reputation in manufacturing cannon and cannonballs, and Turnbull became renowned for his cannonball shot.

When he returned from naval duties, Turnbull joined local side Forth Rangers in nearby Grangemouth. He was quickly spotted by Hibs and invited through to Easter Road in 1947 to meet the inimitable Hibees boss Willie McCartney.

Turnbull was very taken by the 'showy' McCartney, and although he had options to speak with other clubs he was smitten by McCartney's love of Hibernian and dreams of a bright Easter Road future. As well as the dreams there were drams aplenty, and Turnbull always reckoned that his brother, who was in on the transfer negotiations, was as persuaded by the liquid generosity as the prospect of Eddie being a Hibee.

Another local lad, Willie Ormond, also joined Hibs around this time, and the two would travel by bus to Easter Road. As the first official season after the war unfolded, both Turnbull and Ormond made their debuts, and they helped Hibs finish second in the League to Rangers. Pipped for the title by only two points, few could deny that Turnbull had made a telling contribution, nicking a very healthy 13 goals from only 20 outings.

It was a season of so near, yet so far for Hibs. They also reached the Scottish Cup Final by overcoming Motherwell in an epic semi-final. This was in an era of post-war austerity and midweek matches were banned by the government. This ruled out replays and meant matches were played to a finish. It lasted 142 minutes against Motherwell, with 20 minutes of extra-time and then batches of 10 minutes until a goal was scored. Hibernian battled through, only to lose the Final to Aberdeen 2–1. This was the first Final in which players were presented with medals in full view of the crowd. It was a devastating defeat for Hibs, who lost despite being gifted a first-minute strike when the Aberdeen defence presented 'Cubby'' Cuthbertson a goal.

A forceful wing-half, Turnbull established himself in the first team quickly. For many fans he was the linchpin in the Famous Five forward line. While Gordon Smith, Willie Ormond, Bobby Johnstone and Lawrie Reilly were highly skilled, Turnbull earned fame for his strength. This is not to underestimate his skills, but rather to emphasise the key role he played in bringing cohesion to a forward line that was rich in flair but short on muscle.

By 1950 Turnbull had won the first four of his nine international caps. His debut came against Belgium, and he quickly slipped in outings against Switzerland, France and Austria to add to the total. Unfortunately Scotland won only the first of that quartet, and his international career was put on an extended hold.

Turnbull was seldom outshone by his colleagues, and their unique brand

Three cards showing Turnbull's transformation from player (Turf cigarette card) to manager (Dickson and Panini cards)

of attacking football relied heavily on 'Turnbull the enforcer'. He scored the first ever British goal in European football, netting in the 4–0 win over Rot Weiss Essen. Nicknamed 'Ned', he became as famed for his colourful language as his football. Fortunately, in the era before mass television or press coverage, few fans were aware that when he wanted to call a spade a spade he could do so with a surprisingly inventive use of Anglo-Saxon. Nevertheless, he was adored by his teammates, several of whom suggested to me that beneath the occasionally gruff exterior beat a very kind heart indeed.

Turnbull and his cohorts first played as a fivesome in April 1949. The game in question was a friendly in the little village of Sanquar where Hibs squared up to Nithsdale Wanderers. An 8–1 rout followed, and Turnbull helped himself to two goals. Clearly a physically impressive man, he had the happy knack of possessing both aggression and creatively, so much so that Manchester United made tentative enquiries.

There were many highlights for Turnbull as a Hibs player. In 1950 he scored a hat-trick in a League Cup semi-final against Queen of the South, but Motherwell surprisingly won the Final. Indeed, it was a season in which only Lawrie Reilly scored more goals for Hibs. However, Turnbull stole all the headlines in February 1950 when he famously scored four against Celtic, including that rare feat of three from the penalty spot.

It wasn't the only time Turnbull hit four in a game. Gordon Smith's testimonial match against Manchester United in September 1952 turned into one of the greatest football matches ever seen in Edinburgh. Hibs romped home 7–3, and he wrote his name over proceedings in grabbing no fewer than four goals. In 1956 he scored hat-tricks against Motherwell and Dunfermline, which was a fine recovery in a campaign that began with a humiliating 6–1 defeat at Tynecastle in the first game of the season.

For all the Famous Five enthused Scottish football fans, they were undoubtedly a better League team than a Cup side. They won the title three times but failed to land either of the domestic Cup competitions. In 1950–51, for example, they lost in the League Cup Final and Scottish Cup semi-final. There seemed to be a Cup jinx on this fine side, but they did win the League with some style. They retained the League title and were close to making it three consecutive titles. What they excelled in was scoring, and Turnbull contributed his share. His haul of 148 League goals in 349 matches would put many dedicated forwards to shame.

The era of the Famous Five eventually ended on 29 January 1955, when the five played in a 3–2 defeat against Clyde. A month later Bobby Johnstone was transferred to Manchester City for £22,000, and a golden period in Hibs history was over.

Hibs record in the Scottish Cup remained woeful throughout the period of the Famous Five and beyond. There was one notable occasion when Hibs came up against Hearts in a Scottish Cup tie. It was a fifth-round tie in the 1955 competition and pitched the Famous Five against Hearts 'Terrible Trio'. Over 45,000 crammed into Tynecastle expecting to see a close-fought affair, and for quarter of an hour that was exactly what they got.

However, Hibs, in their true Scottish Cup style, collapsed when they conceded a 17th-minute goal. Hearts trio of Conn, Bauld and Wardaugh went to town and by quarter to five had administered a humiliating 5–0 thrashing to Hibs. Lawrie Reilly recalled the game with some resignation in later years.

The Sunday Post, February 11, 1951.   15

AFTER three years as holders, Rangers are out of the Scottish Cup. And odds are the Ibrox club will now end the season without a single major trophy in their possession. Changed days, indeed.

On a no-surprise day victorious Hibs were joined by Aberdeen, Clyde, Celtic, Hearts, Motherwell, Ayr United, Raith Rovers, and Dundee. Only one tie is still alive, Morton v. Airdrie. Replay is at Broomfield on Wednesday.

There will be only two ties in the third round a fortnight hence — Hearts v. Celtic (all-ticket), Morton or Airdrie v. Clyde.

How Hibs Wrote A New Page For Their History Book

RANGERS 2, HIBS 3.   (Half-time—1-1.)

Scorers:—Rangers—Simpson (4, 47 min.); Hibs—Smith (40 min.), Ormond (75 min), Johnstone (81 min.).

HIBERNIAN FOOTBALL CLUB was formed away back in 1875. During their long history they've had some great teams. They've figured in some great games. They've had some great results.

But, for the official record, this must go down as Hibs' greatest performance.

From start to finish, this perfect cup-tie was a ferment of excitement.

Rangers scored early, and for quite a spell it looked as if the Light Blues were going to tear this Easter Road "team of the year" to shreds.

But Hibs steadied. And, with the steadying, came the equaliser. Still not yet the perfect Hibs, they rocked a wee bit once more—and went behind again.

But again they steadied themselves. Again they snatched the equaliser. And, from then onwards, these Hibs burst forth in all their glory, helped themselves to the winning goal, and rounded off the whole show with such brilliance no team in Britain could have stood out against them.

Rangers are out of the cup simply because Hibs found the secret of how to score goals against the best defence in the country. Trap a ball before shooting anywhere near goal and the chance is lost. Bring the ball into a scoring position and smack it first-time—and goals will come.

Here it must be said Hibs' forwards got plenty of the ball to try out all sorts of defence-splitting manoeuvres.

As the game progressed the Easter Road wing-halves, Buchanan and Gallacher, rightly decided there was no necessity to keep a close watch on Thornton and Rae. So they came right upfield to give Hibs five all-star forwards and two semi-forwards.

What happened to Rangers' front line after quarter of an hour is a mystery. During those fifteen minutes, Waddell was at his mightiest. Simpson was holding the line beautifully. Some of Rae's moves

By JACK HARKNESS

reminded me of Bob M'Phail. And Paton was proving himself a more than useful winger.

But all this lasted only for fifteen minutes.

From then on the line became five units. Some of them, in fact, half units. So when Hibs' devastating surge did come, we found Rangers' team, as a force, consisted of Brown, Young, Shaw, Cox, and Woodburn.

And, believe me, King Canute had an easier task trying to keep out the tide than these five gallant Rangers had in stemming this Hibernian onslaught.

It's fitting this classic Cup-tie should have been topped by five classic goals.

In four minutes, Simpson smacked home a perfect Waddell cross. Reckoning on history and forgetting about Hibs, we settled back prepared for the old, old story. Rangers, with a goal in the bag, putting up the shutters.

But an electric Smith-Ormond move ended with Gordon first-timing an unsaveable shot past Brown.

Rangers got off to another flying start immediately after the interval. Simpson showed perfect marksmanship in booting a cross from Paton past Younger.

Then Turnbull's equaliser. A goal in a million. Eddie was standing about 20 yards out on the right when a cross came over from Ormond. Without a fraction's hesitation, Eddie drew back his right foot and hurled a glorious, swerving shot away into the right-hand corner.

And then Johnstone's winner. A free kick against Woodburn just outside the penalty area. The usual solid wall of Rangers players. Turnbull's long run, as if he intended putting that ball clean through anyone who tried to stop it.

But Eddie merely tapped the ball to the unmarked Johnstone at his left. And, with a cut chip shot, Bobby placed the ball clean over the wall of players and right into the top left-hand corner.

Highlights Galore

Talk about pandemonium hindering the players! These Hibs lads knew they'd been twice behind. Knew they had twice draw*n* level. Now they knew they were at last in front. And, most important of all, each and every one knew they had the necessary ability to stay there.

All this, surely, was running through their minds as they slapped, clapped, and descended en masse on Johnstone with their congratulations.

The game just teemed with highlights. The high standard of goalkeeping. Those two terrible misses by Willie Thornton when he was clean through. That let-off for Hibs when Gallacher was lucky to be on the ref.'s blind side when he handled well inside the penalty area.

There was Cox getting his name taken for a tackle on Reilly. And Johnstone getting booked in the closing minutes for what I thought was a bit of time wasting.

There was the tremendous admiration for the way Young, Shaw, Woodburn, and Cox manfully tried to rise to the occasion; and, by some miracle, accomplish the impossible.

And there was Hibs. Jock Govan perhaps lost an odd mark for impetuosity, but all over this was a really grand side. Buchanan's forcing. Gallacher's perfect passing. Paterson's stubbornness. Smith taking the right-wing laurels. Johnstone, Reilly, Turnbull, and Ormond—yes, all that devastating attack doing their bit in the greatest manner.

As I said at the beginning, a performance not bettered, I'm sure, by any Hibs team over the past 76 years.

Rangers—Brown; Young, Shaw; M'Coll, Woodburn, Cox; Waddell, Thornton, Simpson, Rae, Paton.

Hibs—Younger; Govan, Ogilvie; Buchanan, Paterson, Gallacher; Smith, Johnstone, Reilly, Turnbull, Ormond.

Referee—J. A. Mowatt, Glasgow.

In season 1950–51 Hibernian achieved one of their best ever Scottish Cup wins, beating the famous Rangers team 3–2 at Ibrox. This match report tells the full story in glowing terms, but mistakenly credited Ormond with Turnbull's second goal.

'We didn't play well, perhaps the Famous Five was past its best by this point. Certainly Bobby Johnstone left not long afterwards. Nothing went for us in the game, and although we had early chances we didn't take them and then found ourselves chasing the game.'

In 1958 they reached another Final, only to lose to Clyde. Much hinged on the absence of Lawrie Reilly. It ought to have been his final game as a Hibee but a bout of tonsillitis deprived him of the chance to bow out in style, and although Turnbull gave his all he was destined to collect another runners'-up medal.

1958 was also a World Cup year, and Scotland qualified for the Finals in Sweden. Turnbull did not play in the qualifiers and at 35 was the oldest player in the final 22. Recalled after an astonishing eight-year gap, he helped organise training and played in all three matches. In the opening game versus Yugoslavia he had a hand in the first goal Scotland scored in any World Cup Finals competition. He was the ideal inclusion in the squad, having played in Europe with Hibs and closely studied the continental game.

Widely recognised as one of the few Scotland successes at the Swedish World Cup Finals, Turnbull was asked to captain the Scottish League against their English counterparts in October 1958. His coaching credentials were becoming increasingly impressive. In 1959 he swapped the first-team playing jersey for a coaching tracksuit at Easter Road. This wasn't a real surprise as he had shown an interest in doing so for some time.

Much as he was content as a member of the Easter Road back-room staff, there was no way the fiery Turnbull could resist the offer to coach Glasgow's Queen's Park. He was extremely committed while in charge of the Hampden Park amateurs and as a keen student of the game even visited Germany to widen his knowledge of coaching techniques.

It was in season 1963–64 that Turnbull began coaching Queen's Park. The Spiders were unique in Scotland, not only as an amateur club in the Scottish League, but as the only club who employed a coach rather than a manager.

During the 1964–65 season another notable feature in the Scottish scene was the demise of Aberdeen, who had won the title a decade earlier. In February 1965, following a calamitous Cup defeat at East Fife, Tommy Pearson resigned.

The man charged with resurrecting the fortunes of the Granite City club was Eddie Turnbull.

Turnbull's credentials were impeccable when he left the Spiders in 1964–65. The previous season he had steered them to seventh in the Second Division. When he departed they were well on their way to being fourth, but they won just one of their last seven League games, and had Turnbull stayed then they might have earned promotion.

Goalkeeper Bobby Clark was the mainstay of that Queen's Park side. They had pushed Celtic all the way in the Scottish Cup, with the Bhoys fortunate to eke out a 1–0 win at Hampden and it was this passion that Aberdeen wanted.

Aberdeen had no doubts about Turnbull's abilities to succeed Tommy Pearson. He quickly imposed his mark on Pittodrie, the Don's first ever track-suited manager releasing 17 players within weeks of arriving. The season rolled on, and Aberdeen not only climbed the League table but reached the Scottish Cup Final, only to go down narrowly to Celtic. His progress at Pittodrie brought the SFA calling, but he resisted their overtures to become Scotland boss. Goalkeeper Bobby Clark had followed Turnbull from Hampden Park to Pittodrie, and he had no doubt he had made the right move.

'Turnbull was, in my opinion, the man with the finest footballing brain in Scotland. The players loved him, but if you got on the wrong side of him then he could be ruthless. He was a great coach, and it was a sad day when he left Aberdeen. However, his wife hadn't settled in the North-East, and I suppose as an ex-Hibee the lure of going back when Tom Hart began pumping money into the Edinburgh club was too much. But I enjoyed the time we had together in Aberdeen.'

In 1970 the Dons did win the Scottish Cup, and in some style, doing so against the odds when they beat a powerful Celtic team 3–1 at Hampden. Prior to that Final, he referred to Jock Stein, the revered Celtic boss, as 'big eat the breed'. This irreverence had the Dons players in fits of laughter and showed that Turnbull feared no foe and could lighten the mood in tense settings. There was a healthy rivalry and mutual respect between the two, but Turnbull believed himself to be the superior coach. Again Bobby Clark noted the drive and confidence that was making him such a good coach.

'Eddie was years ahead of his time. I was lucky to have him as my mentor in my early days. I had played under him at Queen's Park, and he treated me well. He was keen that I finish my education before concentrating solely on football, and I think he adopted the same approach at Hibs with Tony Higgins.'

It was the ebullient Tom Hart who convinced Turnbull that he should return to Hibernian in July 1971. Hart, who had made his fortune in the building industry, had taken control of Hibs in the early 1970s and quickly recognised that falling attendances and income were seriously hampering the club's ambitions. He saw the two priorities as pumping cash into the club – which he did with a £250,000 injection – and recruiting a talented manager. Turnbull was as outspoken as Hart himself, and thus a perfect partnership was born.

Turnbull got off to a fine start as Hibs boss. He steered the club to the League Cup quarter-finals, and they won their opening League game of the season 2–0 at Hearts. This was a start that bought him time. With his ability in the transfer market, it was all he needed. Among those recruited were Alan Gordon and Alex Edwards, and despite the small sums involved both players became key parts of his wonderful side in the early 70s.

The season ended with Hibs beating Rangers in the 1872 Scottish Cup semi-final, only to lose disastrously to Celtic 6–1 in the Final, a game that has entered folklore as 'the Dixie Deans Final'. However, Hibs learned from the experience. The following season started with Hibs scaling the heights.

They won the Dryburgh Cup (a pre-season tournament) by beating Celtic in the August Final 5–3, this despite a pitch invasion by Celtic fans when Hibs stormed into an impressive 3–0 lead.

Then on 9 December Hibs beat Celtic again, this time in the Scottish League Cup Final, and far easier than the 2–1 scoreline suggested. In Hibernian's next home game they not only paraded the Cup before the match but ran out convincing 8–1 winners against luckless Ayr United. Something good was stirring at Easter Road.

The apex of this purple patch came on New Year's Day 1973. In the Edinburgh derby Hibs went into the match in second place with only Hearts above them. The result sent shockwaves around Scottish football... Heart of Midlothian 0, Hibernian 7. It was a scarcely credible score and gave Hibs the most famous win in their history.

Yet Turnbull craved perfection and refused to rest on his laurels. Remarkably, by the end of the season he was losing faith in his brilliantly attractive side. A European Cup-winners' Cup quarter-final defeat in the Yugoslavian town of Split convinced him that his team lacked the 'bottle' to make the transformation from nearly men to all conquering victors.

Perhaps Turnbull was too quick to condemn his team. The following season they started off in fine form again and retained the Dryburgh Cup by beating Celtic 1–0 at Hampden. The goalscorer was number nine Alan Gordon, who gave Turnbull one of his greatest quotes. Bemused and wearied by Gordon's continual interrupting of a team talk, he responded by shouting 'The trouble wi' you son is that yir brains are all in yir heed'. He dearly wanted his players to let their feet do their talking.

Hibs were unlucky to go out of Europe in 1973 to Don Revie's all-conquering Leeds United side, and shortly afterwards they lost a tight League Cup semi-final to Rangers. Even in the League they finished a close second to Celtic. Here was a good side that was desperately close to being the number one team in Scotland, but Turnbull broke it up too sharply.

Having said that, Hibs had been a 'selling club' for some time, and the loss of the likes of Joe Baker, Neil Martin, Alex Cropley, and Peter Marinello had proved that. However, when Turnbull broke the side up he did so in style. By adding Joe Harper to the Hibernian squad, he signed a player whom he had also recruited at Aberdeen (in October 1969 for a record Aberdeen fee).

Harper was as much an Aberdeen legend as Turnbull and had scored in the 1970 Scottish Cup Final win over Celtic. A ruthless and accomplished finisher, Harper was delighted to team up with him again.

'Eddie displayed all his knowledge when Aberdeen beat Celtic in the 1970 Final. Eddie knew that Celtic's weakness was their defence. He went with two speedy youngsters in Arthur Graham and Derek McKay on the wings and myself and Jim Forrest lying deep. It was the first time I had been involved in anything tactical and it worked a treat. Thanks to Eddie's genius we won 3–1 against a side that was one of the strongest in Europe. Turnbull was a great admirer of good sides and would tell us that this was what we had to strive for.'

Turnbull holds aloft the Dryburgh Cup with two of his favourite players – Pat Stanton (left) and Alan Gordon (right).

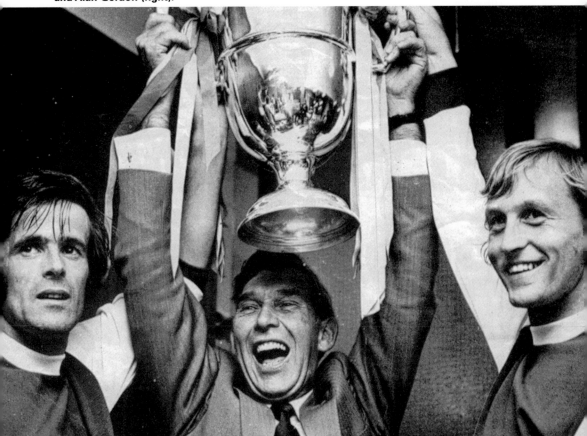

Mind you, Harper almost never re-united with Turnbull at all. When he came back to Scotland from Everton it was touch and go as to where he would end up:

'I wanted to come back to Scotland, and I thought it was going to be to Aberdeen. Everton had accepted a bid from the Dons, but Eddie was keen to sign me and upped the Hibs offer. Eddie knew I was a winner, and he wanted that in his players. You had to want to win in training, in bounce games, in anything in fact.'

1975–76 brought a big change in Scottish football as the League structure was recast, arguably as a direct result of a meeting chairman Tom Hart had called in 1973 to analyse falling attendances. Gone was the old 16-club top flight, to be replaced by a 10-club top League. With two clubs being relegated, the rate of attrition was frightening. Hibs started well, beating Hearts 1–0 at home, with Turnbull's record buy Joe Harper getting the goal. But Hibs were dreadfully inconsistent thereafter.

Sensationally bundled out of the League Cup by little Montrose, they would lose in the UEFA Cup to Liverpool and in a twice-replayed Scottish Cup quarter-final to Motherwell.

The late 70s certainly saw Hibs unable to recapture the glitz and drive that characterised them earlier in the decade. Yet bizarrely they came so close to ending their awful Scottish Cup hoodoo.

The 1978–79 season started oddly with the strange case of Isak Refvik and Svein Mathieson and their on-off transfer saga capturing headlines. Beaten in the League Cup semi-final, Hibs stuttered and bumbled, but fortunately their season of fits and starts magically allowed the good days to coincide with Scottish Cup action. Turnbull's team brushed aside Dunfermline and Meadowbank before winning a titanic quarter-final clash at Easter Road against Hearts. Two of Turnbull's most trusted players – George Stewart and Gordon Rae – scored the key goals.

Gordon Rae, himself a Hibernian legend, was convinced that Turnbull's tactics were the key to success in the March 1979 clash with Hearts:

'It was a match to remember for several reasons. We played with an orange ball, which was odd for the late seventies, and I scored the winner with a left-foot shot which was even odder. But Eddie was geared up for the game and had me man-marking Drew Busby, the experienced Hearts midfielder. Eddie had identified him as Hearts biggest threat, and he was quite prepared to give me the job of shackling him. I really thought that having overcome Hearts it was going to be our year in the Cup.'

Aberdeen were despatched in the semi-final, and so to a final showdown in Glasgow with Rangers. Two of the most tedious 0–0 draws ever witnessed preceded a thrilling second replay. Alas, despite goals by Higgins, MacLeod and Duncan, Hibs were beaten. Duncan's goal had been a tragic own-goal. For Jackie McNamara, the then captain of Hibs, it was a defeat that Turnbull didn't deserve:

'I played for Jock Stein at Celtic and Eddie Turnbull at Hibs, and in terms of tactics I would say Eddie was the best I worked with. He built a really good team too and the side in the late 70s was the best I ever played in. Unfortunately, losing Des Bremner the following season was the beginning of the end.'

Few could have predicted the calamitous 1979–80 season that lay in store, almost like a hangover to the 1979 Cup Final reversal. Hibs won only one of their opening 15 League games and plunged headlong towards relegation. Even the arrival of George Best could not save Hibernian, and a 5–0 Scottish Cup semi-final defeat to Celtic in April was the final straw for Turnbull. He resigned as manager of Hibs after 34 years in the game and was succeeded by his good friend Willie Ormond.

Turnbull was incredibly robust in his old age and a frequent visitor to Easter Road. However, in February 2006 he collapsed at home in Comely Bank, Edinburgh, and spent some time in Edinburgh's Western General Infirmary recovering from a heart attack.

Something that aided Turnbull's recovery was a decision by the SFA to award caps to players from his era. During his international career, caps were only awarded to players representing Scotland against Wales, Northern Ireland and England. Turnbull was unusual in that all his appearances for Scotland came against overseas countries.

Belatedly, the SFA responded to a clamour by fans to recognise the achievements of some famous old stars. The SFA's David Taylor, in magnanimous mood, said:

'We will award a commemorative Scotland cap to any pre-1975 internationals who did not receive one under the previous system in recognition of their achievement in being selected to represent their country. This is an entirely new initiative by the Scottish FA board of directors that will give a tangible souvenir for those who did not appear in the British Championship. Times have changed, and, although the British Championship was once seen as the highlight of the season, playing for Scotland in any match is a great honour.'

The recipient with most international appearances to miss out on a cap was Eddie Turnbull, who played nine times for Scotland between 1948 and 1958.

One of the all time greats in the Scottish game, Turnbull's belated recognition rekindled memories of a career that gave Hibernian in particular much to be proud of. Here was a man who was forceful and successful as a player and thoughtful and successful as a manager. He may not have been the most flashy member of the Famous Five, but arguably he was the most enduring.

EDDIE TURNBULL factfile

Born: Falkirk, 12 April 1923
Position: Inside-forward
Playing career: Hibernian

Hibs League career:

Season	Games	Goals
1946–47	20	13
1947–48	23	11
1948–49	27	8
1949–50	27	18
1950–51	26	15
1951–52	29	6
1952–53	29	17
1953–54	27	13
1954–55	24	4
1955–56	33	18
1956–57	30	14
1957–58	30	9
1958–59	24	2
Total	349	148

International caps:
One Scotland Schoolboy cap
Scotland B: 1 game
Scottish League: 4 games
Scotland: 9 games

TURNBULL'S CUP TORMENT

1946–47: Plays in the Scottish Cup Final against Aberdeen, having scored for Hibs in the 2–1 semi-final win over Motherwell. Hibs score in the first minute but lose 1–2. Earlier in the season, Hibs lost 0–3 to Rangers in the League Cup semi-final.

1947–48: Hibs reach the Scottish Cup semi-final but are beaten 0–1 by Rangers.

1949–50: Hibs play Dunfermline in the League Cup semi-final at Hearts' Tynecastle Park. Despite a goal from Lawrie Reilly they lost 1–2.

1950–51: Hibs are back at Tynecastle, this time to contest a Scottish Cup semi-final. However, they flop again and are beaten 2–3. Hibs reached the League Cup Final when Turnbull scored a hat-trick in the semi-final against Queen of the South, but they lose the Final to Motherwell 0–3.

1952–53: Hibs reach the League Cup semi-final, but they lose 1–2 to Dundee at Tynecastle Park. Turnbull scores twice in a Coronation Cup semi-final win over Newcastle United (4–0), but they lose the Final at Hampden to Celtic 0–2.

1953–54: Yet again, Hibs lose a League Cup semi-final at Tynecastle Park. This time East Fife are the winners in a thrilling 2–3 match.

1955–56: Hibs reach the semi-final of the inaugural European Cup but lose to French club Stade Rheims.

1957–58: At last another Scottish Cup Final appearance, but Hibs play poorly on the day and Clyde win 1–0.

LAWRIE REILLY

Lawrie Reilly signed for Hibs from Edinburgh Thistle in 1945 and went on to become one of the most feared strikers in Scotland. Yet he actually had difficulty breaking into the Hibs side.

Born and raised in Edinburgh, Reilly cut his teeth at juvenile level with North Merchiston and Edinburgh Thistle before joining Hibs. He made his debut when only 17 but was very much a fringe player when the title went to Easter Road in 1948. In fact, initially Reilly had to be content with playing on the wing. He replaced Willie Ormond, who was ruled out with a broken leg, and made such a good job of being an outside-left that he was capped by Scotland in that position.

Eventually, the more experienced Ormond returned, and Reilly was tried at centre-forward; the rest, as they say, is history. Fortunately Reilly, like colleagues Eddie Turnbull and arguably Gordon Smith, had a basic secret weapon – he could comfortably play in any forward position.

Reilly himself felt that if he was going to make the grade as a professional footballer then the chances were that it would be with Hibs, this despite living just a stone's throw from Tynecastle Park.

'I had followed the Hibs faithfully as a youngster and had probably seen them play in nearly every ground in Scotland. My father and grandfather had both been Hibs fanatics so it was in the family. Mind you, I lived near Tynecastle, and Hearts were actually showing an interest in me when Hibs offered me a contract. I didn't need to be asked twice and had no hesitation in signing.'

Reilly's debut came against Kilmarnock on 4 September 1946, and he scored as Hibs romped to a 6–0 win. In five first-team matches he scored

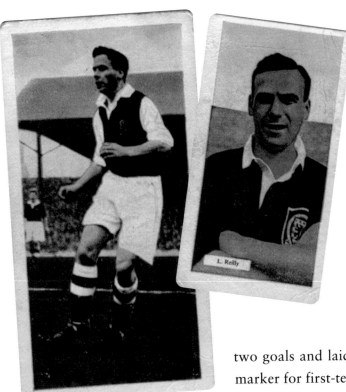

Lawrie Reilly was a Scotland hero, and these cards by Chix and the National Spastics Society show him in his national glory.

two goals and laid down a tentative marker for first-team football. In the 1947–48 season Hibs landed the Championship, and although the young Lawrie was but a bit-player he did score four goals in his six games.

Reilly shone as a centre-forward. In season 1950–51 he scored 23 League goals, and in the next six seasons he netted 27, 30, 15, 15, 23 and 16. He thus became the first Hibs player to top the Easter Road scoring charts in seven consecutive seasons. His haul of 30 League goals in season 1952–53 was a club record at the time.

Looking back on that rich haul of goals, Reilly suggests that a few goals stand out more than all the others.

'There are two goals that I scored that gave me great pleasure. The first was at Fir Park and involved a long run. I evaded four or five Motherwell defenders who, fortunately for me, lunged in rather than jockeying me for position. Finally I had the goalkeeper to beat, and I managed to go round him and knock it home. What stands out in my memory is the way the

Three cards from the 1950s showing the most prolific Hibernian centre-forward of all time – Lawrie Reilly (cards by Barratt, Adventure and Turf cigarettes).

Motherwell supporters applauded me. I think they genuinely enjoyed seeing a good goal, perhaps due to the fact that they had seen a string of good sides in the 1930s.

'My second memory is of a goal against Falkirk. Eddie Turnbull fired over a real thunderbolt of a cross-come-shot, and by some fluke I managed to get my forehead on it and the ball simply rocketed home. I suppose it was a bit like returning a vicious tennis serve. The Bairns 'keeper Bobby Brown didn't even move and actually applauded me before picking the ball out of the net.'

For fans of Hibernian, the above is probably a surprise. Most fans reckoned that his finest showing came on 20 September 1952 when Hibs beat Hearts 3–1 at Easter Road, and Reilly scored a hat-trick. *The Scotsman* was full of praise:

'It was a well deserved hat-trick by a fast and tenacious centre who, once he got the ball, seldom let it go, except to his side's advantage.'

One week later he fired in four in a 7–3 rout of Motherwell at Fir Park. This marked an incredible purple patch for Hibs as they won their first derby in four years and bagged an astonishing 22 goals in just eight days. At this stage Easter Road was becoming a crucible for attacking football.

Physically Reilly was not everyone's idea of the archetypal centre-forward. He was not particularly big, standing at just 5ft 7in, nor was he especially heavy, yet he was undoubtedly a prolific marksman and scored a good number of headers. His explanation was that the other members of the Famous Five delivered telling crosses and passes. Were he less modest, he would have mentioned his own sense of timing and sheer bravery.

The five had come together in April 1949 and soon had the whole country in raptures. As Tom Campbell and Pat Woods noted in their history of Celtic, *Rhapsody in Green*, other players admired Hibs hugely in this era. Alfie Boyd, the captain of Dundee, said 'Against Hibs you take the field with barely suppressed excitement coursing through the team and this lift lasts through the whole game, so that you find yourself getting to the ball from positions which normally appear hopeless.' Hibs, the Celtic historians noted, were 'THE talking point of Scottish football' and became a magnet for neutrals up and down Scotland.

Put simply, they noted that the five were exceptionally talented individually and together, and that Reilly was arguably the most lethal of them all. There was a seemingly irresistible momentum about Hibernian in the early 1950s.

'Smith, Johnstone, Reilly, Turnbull and Ormond: a quintet that adorned the football scene in the post-war seasons, names that could be rhymed off by every schoolboy in the country. At centre, Lawrie Reilly was the quintessential striker; he was the epitome of alertness, skilled with head and feet and never gave defences a moment to relax.'

Quite how the Famous Five came to be so labelled is shrouded in mystery. Reilly himself was at a loss to recall how the name came about, but he did recall that it gave rise to one humorous incident outside Easter Road.

'I honestly can't remember how, or even when, it started. In fact the only Famous Five I ever really knew of was the one in Enid Blyton's kiddies' books! What I can remember is coming out of Easter Road one evening and a group of wee boys running up to us and saying to Willie Ormond "Are you one of the Magnificent Seven?"'

Reilly was at times uneasy with the label Famous Five as he felt it detracted from the good work done by other members of a very good Hibs team.

'I know that Bobby Combe, who could stand in for any of us and was a regular half-back throughout this period, once talked of the Famous Six, and I felt that naming the team the Famous Five was a bit narrow. It seemed to sell the other lads short because we had a great defence and some excellent half-backs. But you know football. We were the ones that grabbed the goals and the headlines, but we were only so good up front because we knew we were sound at the back.'

Even though Hibs, and in particular Reilly, terrorised opposition defences, there was a great deal of respect in the game, and he remains quick to recognise the talents of his former opponents.

'Willie Woodburn of Rangers was a real challenge given his height and strength. However, we devised a strategy against him which was to keep the ball on the deck as often as possible. Willie was a good friend of mine, and I enjoyed our jousts.

'Alec Young and then Jim Clunie at Aberdeen were both stuffy defenders and hard to overcome. Andy Paton at Motherwell was a different challenge altogether as he liked to play cultured football and was unlike any other centre-half. I saw all games as a personal duel between myself and the

Lawrie Reilly is foiled by the St Mirren 'keeper before a packed house at Easter Road.

centre-half, and if I read in the match reports after the game that I had come out on top I was very happy.'

It says much for Reilly's talents that he was able to transfer his considerable domestic successes to the international stage. No Hibs player before or since has been able to match his 38-cap haul, and it seems unlikely that any will ever challenge his 22-goal total. He was loved by Scotland supporters and earned himself a special nickname. He earned the tag 'Last Minute Reilly' due to his uncanny ability to snatch dramatic late goals. Expectations were certainly placed on his shoulders, particularly as he had been Scotland's top scorer for three consecutive seasons. When he scored five goals for Scotland in his five appearances against England at Wembley, he cemented his place in the supporters' affections.

The only blot on his international copy book was missing out on the 1954 World Cup Finals when a bout of pleurisy prevented him from travelling. Mind you, given how badly those Finals went for Scotland (they lost one game to Uruguay 7–0), this was perhaps a fortunate escape. But

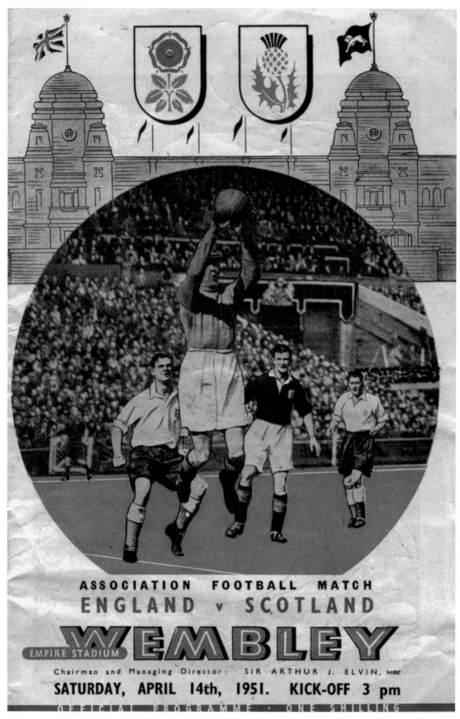

A famous match programme for fans of the Scottish national side. Scotland beat 'The Auld Enemy' 3–2 at Wembley in this thrilling clash, and Lawrie Reilly grabbed one of the goals.

when Reilly did play for Scotland he made an excellent job of the challenge. It was sometimes suggested that Hibs' winger Gordon Smith and Willie Ormond failed to replicate their form in a Scotland jersey, but that charge could never be levelled at Reilly.

Reilly was an international hero and the darling of the Hampden slopes. In his opening 12 matches in dark blue, Scotland won the lot. He had a first-half hat-trick in a 6–0 win over the USA at Hampden Park; little wonder he was a viewed by some as a lucky mascot. But just as he loved the Edinburgh derbies, so he loved the clash of Scotland against England. The joust with the Auld Enemy has long been the most important game on the Scottish football calendar, and Reilly rose to the occasion several times:

'All of the Scotland games at Wembley were special. I played in five games at Wembley and scored five goals.

'In 1949 we were the underdogs, and England had the likes of Wright, Finney and Matthews in their team. Two years later we went back and beat them 3–2. In 1953 I scored a last-minute goal to prevent Scotland losing. That was possibly the game that sealed my "Last Minute Reilly" nickname.

'1955 was a calamity and we were thumped 7–2. The funny thing is we didn't do too badly early on, and when we got back to 2–1 I thought we were going to win. Stanley Matthews confirmed this after the game at the post-match banquet when he let me know he was worried that we were going to complete a magnificent fight-back.

'In my last game we lost 2–1, and I went into the game with an injured foot. I suffered a knock just two days before the game and had to play with stitches in my foot. Although the doctor did a marvellous job in treating the injury, I think it preyed on my mind.'

However, the 'Last Minute' title did rather detract from the real facts which were that Reilly was a handful through the entire 90 minutes. How else could he have bagged no fewer than 22 goals in his 38 internationals? Only three players scored more goals for Scotland – Denis Law, Kenny Dalglish and Hughie Gallacher. Reilly grabbed his goals in an eight-year spell, Law and Dalglish took nearly twice as long and even Gallacher needed 11 years to grab just two goals more than Reilly. Law played 55 games and Dalglish over 100.

Reilly, by his own admission, was but one part of a phenomenally talented forward line. One cannot help but wonder how Scotland would have fared had they tried the entire Famous Five in one international, but it never happened. Bobby 'Nicker' Johnstone, a key element of the Five, once said:

'One of my main regrets in football is that the international selectors never played all five of us in the same team for Scotland.'

All five, bar Turnbull, did play for the Scottish League against their League of Ireland counterparts at Celtic Park in October 1952. The outcome was impressive. Scotland romped home 5–1, and Reilly grabbed no fewer than four of the Scotland goals. In March of the following year he was again the main man. This time the venue was Ibrox and the opposition the more challenging English League side, but it mattered little to him as he banged home the only goal of the game.

Reilly played in 14 Scottish League matches and scored 14 goals. He scored on his debut in September 1948 and kept up a scoring barrage until his last League honour in 1955. Some of those League matches were high profile, and the England game mentioned above attracted a crowd of just under 70,000.

As well as serving Scotland at various levels, Reilly was able to play in Europe with Hibs and his memories of that experience make for interesting reading given the modern obsession with European competition.

'We never realised how big European football would be. It was just an experience then, but once we won one or two games we got a bit more interested. Sadly Rheims knocked us out in the semi-final, or who knows what might have happened.

'My main memory is of the tie we played away to Rott Weiss Essen. The rain simply lashed down and it was a wonder anyone came out to watch the game. The only supporters we had over there were the troops stationed in Germany. Our manager had insisted that we should not attack but restrict Essen to a 0–0 scoreline if possible. To ask Bobby Johnstone, Gordon Smith, or me to do this was not in our make-up, and after 10 minutes we thought "to hang with this". We abandoned the defensive stuff and we beat them 3–0.'

But even the potential glitz of playing in Europe paled into insignificance when compared to an ambitious trip undertaken by Hibs to South America. In the summer of 1953 Hibernian travelled to Brazil, and as Reilly recalls it was an epic journey.

'Hibernian flew to South America... but it was not like modern air travel. We got to Brazil by the following tortuous journey. Flew from Edinburgh to London, London to Paris, Paris to Lisbon, Lisbon to Dakaar, Dakaar to Recife, then on to Rio De Janeiro. Hibernian flew out on Coronation Day, and thanks to the wonders of television we saw the Coronation at every stopping point!'

Hibs prepare for season 1950–51. Back row: J. Paterson, McColl (trainer), A. Buchanan, T. Younger, H. Shaw (manager), J. Govan, J. Ogilvie, J. Souness, S. Kean (assistant trainer), M. Gallacher. Seated: W. Terris (director), L. Reilly, R. Combe, H. Swan (chairman), G. Smith, W. Ormond, T. Hartland (director). Front: R. Johnstone, E. Turnbull.

In what was a poorly documented part of the club's history, Hibernian played all three matches in the mighty Maracana Stadium. It held 200,000 so even with 30,000 in place it looked nearly empty. Throughout their stay Hibs were entertained by the local British Community Club, and without them the club would have been left to their own devices. However, even expert help could not prevent Lawrie Reilly ending up spending two days in a Brazilian hospital. He swallowed sea water when trying to 'ride a wave'. Given the poor reputation of beaches and sea water at that time, he was hospitalised. Two days later he left hospital at lunchtime and played in a match in the evening.

Like many of his contemporary Hibernian players, Reilly picked up several honours. He was twice a League Championship winner, and although he failed to land a Scottish Cup-winners' badge he did play in a League Cup Final. Having said that, he surely deserved to play in more than one Final. He scored in semi-finals against Dundee, Dunfermline and East Fife, yet it was only a semi-final in which he didn't score (against Queen of the South) that Hibs won.

'We didn't have a great record in the League Cup considering the quality of side we had. Against Dunfermline I scored the opening goal, and we lost 1–2, and I also scored against Dundee, and we lost that one too. I thought I had cracked it against East Fife when I scored two, but we still lost 2–3 and we ended up with only 10 men as our injury hoodoo hit again. Maybe I was a menace to my own team: perhaps if I hadn't scored in semi-finals things might have turned out better!'

Eddie Turnbull's hat-trick against Queen of the South in 1950 gave Hibs a Final outing against Motherwell, which unfortunately proved a huge disappointment. Ravaged by injury, Hibs had to field a side that was quite different from their regular 11, and they failed to gel on the day.

All in all, season 1950–51 was a strange one. Hibs won the League with plenty to spare. They finished a full 10 points clear of second-place Rangers and lost only four games in a 30-match League campaign. With 78 goals for and only 26 goals against, they had the best goal record in the League. Yet ninth placed Motherwell denied them two Cup successes. In the League Cup Hibs reached the Final against the Lanarkshire club and were in optimistic mood for the big game. And with good reason. Just two weeks earlier, at Motherwell's Fir Park, Hibs had crushed the Steelmen by a whopping 6–2. Goals by Ormond (2), Johnstone (2), Turnbull and Reilly had the Hibs fans in confident mood, yet in the Final Hibs played horribly and lost 0–3 as Motherwell wreaked a painful revenge.

'We were badly hampered in the run up to the match when we lost Eddie Turnbull. Eddie was the driving force in our forward line. We also had to contend with a little bit of interference when chairman Harry Swan insisted that Willie Ormond played as an inside-left. His thinking was that he had seen Ormond play well in a six-a-side match as an inside-forward! It was incredible, and Hugh Shaw had to go along with the chairman's suggestion. The situation with Ormond and Turnbull was bad enough, but then Harry and Hugh decided to compound things by playing young Jackie Bradley as left-winger. Poor Jackie just froze on the day. Finally, myself and Gordon Smith carried injuries into the game, which we shouldn't have done. So all in all it was a fairly disastrous match.'

When Gordon Smith picked up an early knock (in the days before substitutes), Hibs were pretty well done for. Yet, having said that, they dominated the entire first half and much of the second, before Motherwell scored three times in the final 15 minutes. Young goalkeeper Tommy Younger had a bit of a nightmare and was photographed in tears at the end of a match that saw him concede two soft goals. Thereafter, he was known, especially at Hearts, as the 'Greetin' Goalie'. Lawrie Reilly, for once, was shackled, the unconventional Andy Paton giving him little to feed on. As the *Sunday Post* noted, the final straw came with the third goal.

'In the last minute Tommy Younger meant to clear. He kicked the ground and the ball hit his shin, to run straight to Watters. The winger, despite his amazement, whisked the ball back over Younger's head into the empty goal.'

This was the mistake that finally left Younger distraught, and when the match ended the Motherwell goalkeeper John Johnston ignored his teammates to make his way up the field to put his arms round the disconsolate young Hibs 'keeper.

On Monday 15 December 1958 Reilly was given a well-deserved testimonial against an international select at Easter Road. On reflection, a meeting with Rangers might have been more fitting. Between 1946 and 1953 only two teams had won the Scottish Championship. Rangers had taken four and the other three went to Hibernian. It was a clash of opposites. Rangers were known for their 'Iron Curtain' defence, while Hibs were famous for attacking football. The 1953 title race was the tightest, Rangers edging home on goal average.

Reilly certainly knew that he had played in a very special era for Scottish football. One match against Hearts attracted the club's record crowd, and he recalled the day with awe in later years:

'The crowd were packed in so tightly that they couldn't move to get a cigarette out of their pockets. That was the sort of interest football generated in the post-war era, and we at Hibs were very lucky that so many good players ended up at the same place at the same time. Hibs were treated like kings around 1950, and we didn't fear anyone.'

His contemporaries were full of praise for Reilly. I remember speaking to Gordon Smith about him, and his version was complimentary in the extreme.

'Lawrie took his opportunity in football with both hands (or should I say feet!) He really enjoyed his football, he was so good in the air. He was

Lawrie Reilly, Gordon Smith, Willie Ormond's widow, Bobby Johnstone and Eddie Turnbull at the official opening of the the Famous Five stand in 1998.

not the quickest player over a distance, but when close up and taking a man on he was very quick. He was in the same class as Stanley Matthews, very clever and awfully good at close quarters.'

Reilly's career, while lengthy, was actually cut short, and he was forced to retire when aged only 29. What would have evolved if he had been around as Joe Baker made his breakthrough into the Hibs side?

Of all the players I ever interviewed, Reilly was perhaps the most lucid. His memory of matches some 50 years ago was incredibly accurate. Here was a man who not only enjoyed a wonderful career but had the good fortune to recall it in the most minute and engaging detail. A lovely person to talk to, Reilly was a modest as could be. A one club man and a national hero, he is perhaps the greatest Hibee of them all.

LAWRIE REILLY factfile

Born: Edinburgh, 28 October 1928

Position: Centre-forward

Playing career: Hibernian

Hibs League career:

Season	Games	Goals
1946–47	5	2
1947–48	6	4
1948–49	20	14
1949–50	29	16
1950–51	29	23
1951–52	29	27
1952–53	28	29
1953–54	18	15
1954–55	20	15
1955–56	29	23
1956–57	26	17
1957–58	14	2
Total	253	187

International caps:

Scottish League: 14 games, 14 goals

Scotland: 38 games, 22 goals

HIBERNIAN'S GOALSCORING HEROES

Player	Career	Apps	Goals
L. Reilly	1946–58	253	187
E. Turnbull	1946–59	349	148
W. Ormond	1946–61	348	133
G. Smith	1946–59	310	126
J. Baker	1957–61 & 1970–72	158 (1)	113
R. Johnstone	1948–55 & 1959–61	195	100
J. O'Rourke	1962–74	202 (8)	81
P. Cormack	1962–70 & 1979–81	197 (3)	77
A. Duncan	1969–84	436 (12)	73
A. MacLeod	1974–84	201 (7)	72

LAWRIE REILLY... goals at Wembley

1949 England 1, Scotland 3 (Mason, Steel, Reilly)

1951 England 2, Scotland 3 (Johnstone, Reilly, Liddell)

1953 England 2, Scotland 2 (Reilly 2)

1955 England 7, Scotland 2 (Reilly, Docherty)

JOE BAKER

The phrase 'Hibernian legend' could easily have been coined with Joseph Henry Baker in mind. How else do you categorise a career that brought goals, goals and yet more goals? There were times when young Joe Baker's exploits at Easter Road read like an adventure from a *Boys' Own* magazine article, indeed, with striker Joe, fact could be more outlandish than fiction.

In season 1959–60 Baker scored a staggering 42 League goals from just 33 matches for Hibernian. He was the first player from outside the English League to be capped for England. His exploits brought him 100 goals both north and south of Hadrian's Wall, and between times he played in the Italian League. He once scored nine goals in a Scottish Cup tie, and he racked up 14 Hibernian hat-tricks. But such facts, amazing as they are, mask the sheer physical excitement of his career. Here was the classic charismatic number nine, a player whom the fans could relate to with ease. With his film-star looks, wonderful ability and boy-next-door quality, he was loved by all who met him.

Baker was born in Liverpool to an English father and Scottish mother. His dad was serving in the navy at the time, hence the fact that his brother Gerry (who also served Hibernian for a spell) was born in New York. His parents married in the US but returned to Merseyside when World War Two broke out. Liverpool was targeted by

A young Baker featured in this children's sweet cigarette card.

the Luftwaffe, and the young Baker family upped sticks and headed for the maternal home of Motherwell. His place of birth however was to deny Scotland one of the finest centre-forwards reared north of the border. As Baker himself wistfully recalled:

'I was only six weeks old when my parents moved to Motherwell and Gerry was just two. However, at that time you could only play for the nation of your birth, so Gerry was destined to be a United States international, and I went on to play for England.'

Thus both Baker boys were lost, and the loss of Joe echoed that of Bobby Ferrier, the great Motherwell player of the 1930s. Ferrier spent his entire senior career with Motherwell and made over 600 Scottish League appearances, indeed he even played for the Scottish League, but it was to no avail as he could only play for England having been born in Sheffield.

Joe Baker was a hugely talented schoolboy footballer, so much so that he was capped twice by Scotland at that level. The inconsistent rulings of the time meant that Schoolboy caps could be awarded to resident pupils regardless of their place of birth.

The Baker boys were blossoming into fine footballers, and a string of scouts beat a path to their door. Ted Drake, then manager of Chelsea, pipped them all in 1955 by offering Gerry a place at Championship-winning Chelsea, and Joe travelled with him as a companion. Given a chance in trial games, Joe shone, but he unfortunately became homesick pretty quickly and returned to central Scotland after only six weeks in west London.

Baker settled in to an engineering apprenticeship and reverted to playing juvenile football. Spotted by the talent scouts while representing Craigneuk Boys Club, he was persuaded to sign schoolboy forms with Hibernian, and they arranged that he should spend time with junior club Armadale Thistle with a view to toughening him up. There he linked up with Johnny MacLeod and the two would take their Armadale connection back to Easter Road with some verve. Baker was with Armadale barely a season before being 'called up' by Hibs and steadily thrust into first-team action.

'Hibs had been very clever and invited me along to Easter Road when I was only 15 as a guest to see Hibs play Rhiems in the European Cup. At that stage I was an impressionable youngster, and as I watched this game I was just amazed at the football that was being played, by both Hibs and Rhiems. That was me hooked on Easter Road; I've been in love with the club ever since.

'I recall that not long after I had made a few reserve appearances I was given my debut at Airdrie in a midweek game, in place of the great Lawrie Reilly. Unfortunately, I only got to play a handful of games with Lawrie before his knees packed up.'

That debut was in a League Cup tie on 15 August 1957. A couple of months later, in a home match against Queen's Park, Baker scored both Hibs goals in a 2–0 win. Shortly afterwards he bagged three in a friendly against Tottenham, and a glorious hat-trick against St Mirren in early November signalled that a new kid on the block had well and truly made his mark. He was a teenage sensation, and he quite simply exploded on to the Scottish football scene. The season ended with him having made 25 League appearances, scoring 14 goals. It would be fair to say that a very modest Hibs team would have been relegated were it not for his youthful input.

Joe Baker had film-star good looks.

If the League had been a struggle that term, then, by contrast, the Scottish Cup had been a blessed release. Hibs beat Dundee United in the third round after a replay, Baker scoring in a 2–0 win. The next round sent them across the city to face Hearts. Edinburgh was buzzing with excitement, a local derby in the Cup and in a season that was seeing Hearts run away with the title. How good were Hearts? Well, they won the

League by a clear 13 points from Rangers (in an era of only two points for a win), and they scored an astounding 132 goals in their 34 League games. Only once that season would Hearts lose a League game.

But Hearts lost that Scottish Cup tie to Hibs, and they lost for one simple reason… Joe Baker. As their favourites won a mesmerising Cup tie 4–3 at Tynecastle, 1 March 1958 became a red-letter day for Hibernian fans, and in Joe Baker they had a new hero as he scored all four Hibs goals.

Baker scored in the 22nd, 28th, 66th and 81st minutes. It was an astonishing display for a 17-year-old. His first goal came when Willie Ormond's shot rebounded from a post. Number two came when a pass from Johnny Grant sent him through to shoot past Marshall, but Hearts equalised shortly after half time. Not long after the hour mark, he completed his hat-trick, and his goal with nine minutes left finally won a seven-goal thriller.

Accolades poured in after the game. Lawrie Reilly, who had watched from the stand, said:

'Watching Joe score all four in that game remains one of my happiest footballing memories. I don't think I ever enjoyed a game more, and you have to say that Joe more or less won that game on his own. Lawrie Leslie, in goal, had a great game, but on the day Joe was the reason Hibs won.'

Hibs battled on to the Scottish Cup Final only to fall meekly to Clyde in a poor Hampden Final. Hampered by injury and with the teenage Baker a pale shadow of his usual self, it was a depressing end to a season that had offered a first Cup win since 1902. Baker's only noteworthy contribution on a disappointing day was to punch home a cross, an act spotted by an eagle-eyed official. Ironically, had he done this in the modern game he would have been sent off.

The following season Hibs struggled again and were heavily indebted to Baker for their survival. This time he hit a purple patch mid-season that yielded 16 goals in a nine-match spell. In 26 League games he scored 25 goals. His form was such that England introduced him to their Under-23 side, giving him his debut on 24 September 1958 in Sheffield against Poland, and he would collect five awards at this level while with Hibs.

In season 1959–60 Baker exhausted football writers up and down Scotland with his exploits. By any standards he was fulfilling all of the early promise he had shown. Where were the superlatives to allow a calm observation of a young centre-forward who scored 42 League goals in only 33 starts? Twice Hibs scored 10 or more goals in a League game. The total of 106 goals in the campaign was more than any other club in the League, but city rivals Hearts once again took the Championship.

By 1959 Baker was showing so much talent that the full England side beckoned. Amid great controversy on 18 November 1959, he was capped against Northern Ireland at Wembley. Nothing could halt his natural confidence, and he scored a typically emphatic strike from 25 yards on what was a sumptuous debut. As he noted:

'That goal really helped me and won the crowd over. But I never truly settled with the England squad or felt accepted by the media. In fact, on my very first trip to the England training camp I told the taxi driver that I was going to play for England, and he grew very suspicious of me on account of my strong Scottish accent. Convinced that I was intent on harming the England squad, he radioed the police, and we were soon pulled over by a panda car. It was only when the police got through to England boss Walter Winterbottom that they realised I was genuinely a Scot on my way to play with England! People would later ask me what part of England I came from, and I would say "Wishaw!" I became known as England's Scottish player.'

Clearly, by 1960–61 everyone either knew about the Fabulous Baker Boy or would shortly know of him. But no one, it seemed, could stop him. The Third Lanark defenders certainly couldn't, and the Glasgow club conceded five to Baker as Hibs romped home 8–4. But five was small compared to what happened on 11 February 1961 in a Scottish Cup tie against non-League Peebles Rovers. On that wintry afternoon he went into overdrive and scored nine as Hibs romped home 15–1.

It was a story from heaven for the press writers of the day because it linked him to his brother Gerry in a bizarre tale of scoring excess. Joe Baker himself summed the story up beautifully.

'Against Peebles Rovers I remember that in the run-up to the game their centre-half was in the national press saying what he would do to stop me. That rankled a bit, and I had five goals before half time. The papers after the game talked of the Baker Boy almost getting a Baker's dozen.

'The remarkable thing was that my brother Gerry had scored 10 for St Mirren against Glasgow University the previous season and my haul came in the very next season. That meant that a pair of brothers had scored 19 goals in two Scottish Cup games. For the life of me I can't ever imagine that being done again.'

Hibs remained an enigma. Again they failed to land any silverware, and yet they reached the semi-finals of the Fairs Cup. And that European competition gave Baker a new stage to impress on.

In the second round the Edinburgh men defeated the mighty Barcelona, with Baker scoring twice in the Nou Camp (during a 4–4 draw) and once in the decisive 3–2 win at Easter Road. Barcelona knew all about the dangerous Hibs number nine, so, in a lovely, simple piece of

By the time Baker joined Nottingham Forest he was thicker set but worldly-wise.

deception, Hibs had Baker swap his jersey, and he wore the number-eight top for the game. By the time Barcelona twigged what was going on, Baker had hit the goal trail. He was certainly the kind of player who thrived in those matches:

'It was a break from the general domestic games. You knew everyone at home and knew the way they would play. The continentals played a different kind of football; they held the ball, had different tactics and it was a learning process for a Scottish team.

'My favourite memory must be the Barcelona game when we beat them 3–2 at Easter Road. We had drawn 4–4 in Barcelona and the tension was high in Edinburgh. The game turned on the penalty the referee awarded us. The Barcelona team simply "lost the plot" and laid into the referee. Had they done it today, they would have been banned from Europe for years.'

The semi-finals followed, and Hibs drew twice with Italian aces Roma. Baker scored in both matches, getting a brace in the match in the Italian capital. Once more the British footballing press sat up and took notice, but this time they were joined by eager Italian football clubs. Baker, who had played for England Under-23s against Italy at Newcastle in November, was now firmly in the sights of leading Serie A clubs. Although Hibs lost the semi-final play-off by a whopping 6–0 in Italy, the die was already cast for Baker and a deal to take him to Torino signed and sealed. Hibs raked in what was then a huge fee of £73,000.

Several Italian clubs had been vying for Baker's signature, and Fiorentina had been among the more persistent. However, Torino were a club with a proud history and rich tradition. Based in the northern city of Turin, they had strode like a giant over Italian football in the mid to late 1940s, winning five consecutive titles, until their period of dominance was cruelly ended by the dreadful Superga air crash when their entire team was wiped out.

They were relegated in 1959 but had bounced back instantly and were intent on re-establishing themselves in the top flight again. This required some lavish spending, and hence they bought Denis Law from Manchester City and Baker from Hibs in a bold move. There was something ironic in Baker signing for a club nicknamed 'the Maroons', a title they shared with Hibs' great Edinburgh rivals Hearts.

Of course, the loss of such a talent was keenly felt by the Hibs supporters. While Baker had wanted a £5 wage increase on his £12 weekly basic, he hadn't specifically asked to move from Edinburgh, and had Hibs met his wage demand then he, like Reilly and Turnbull before him, might have spent his entire career in green and white.

The departure of the talismanic 21-year-old left a gaping hole in the Hibs side, one that the club had no realistic chance of filling, and it was the *Edinburgh Evening News*' football writer who summed up best what Hibs had lost.

'Joe Baker was a one-man goal machine, with two good feet, great pace, and excellent ability in the air. He brought a combination rarely seen in the modern game and his terrific acceleration and non-stop style bothered every defence he faced.'

Baker's move to Torino in May 1961 united him with the equally popular and lively Scotland striker Denis Law. That partnership should have terrorised Italian defences but in truth their moves never really worked out. The defensive system that was prevalent in Italy worked against the natural flair that both Baker and Law thrived on, and the physical nature and darker side of the Italian game ground both players down.

Nonetheless, there were high spots. For Baker the biggest of these surely came on 1 October 1961 as he scored the only goal in a typically keenly contested Turin derby between Torino and their fierce rivals Juventus. The fans in the Stadio delle Alpi were won over, and when Law quickly raced to a total of 10 League goals it seemed that the good days might be about to unfold for Torino once more.

Alas it was not to be, and in February 1962 Baker had a serious car

crash. Law, his passenger (and flatmate), was injured, but Baker sustained serious injuries that confined him to hospital for weeks and were initially life-threatening. It further soured his Italian experience, and in the summer he returned to Britain.

It was Arsenal who rescued him. Billy Wright, the former Wolves and England star, was cutting his teeth at managerial level and made Joe Baker his first major signing. Amid much publicity in the summer of 1962, still aged just 22, Baker signed for the North London giants.

Arsenal, who had to stump up £67,500, and Baker were a perfect match. While it was true that he failed to land any honours as a Gunner, he did re-establish his professional standing. He scored on his debut against Orient and went on to be the Arsenal top scorer that season, and in every season he spent at Highbury. His 29 League goals in 1962–63 were only bettered by his good friend Jimmy Greaves (also returned from Italy), who stuck away 37 for rivals Spurs.

Joe Baker would grab 93 goals in only 144 League matches for Arsenal, and 101 goals when Cup matches were included. As a result, he became one of the first players to notch a century of goals on both sides of the border.

'I scored around 100 goals for Arsenal and really enjoyed my time at Highbury. Looking back, the only regret I have is that I never won a medal during my time in North London.'

Arguably, it was typical of Baker to underestimate his contribution. But statistics mattered little to the fans of the day. Rather it was the style that Baker brought to Highbury that fans relished as much as his scoring. His wonderful acceleration over short distances, powerful heading and razor-sharp penalty-box reactions endeared him to the adoring North Bank; explosive would be the one word summary.

Baker was also a passionate player, and on one occasion the fiery side of his game got the better of him. The match in question was against Liverpool, who boasted a Herculean-like centre-half in the fearsome

Scotsman Ron Yeats. When tempers frayed at Highbury, blows were exchanged, and to the general amazement of everyone present Baker succeeded in flooring the Liverpool man whom Bill Shankly had dubbed 'my colossus'.

Such scuffles were rare, however, and Baker was happiest using his 5ft 7in frame to terrorise defences in a wholly legitimate fashion. He bagged five in one memorable thrashing of Everton, and a hat-trick against deadly rivals Tottenham cemented his standing with the Highbury faithful. The icing on the cake was the resurrection of his international career.

'In the winter of 1965–66 I played in three games for England and scored two goals. I was in the 40-strong pool that Alf Ramsey named in the run up to the 1966 World Cup Finals, and it was only the strong form of men like Geoff Hurst, Jimmy Greaves, Bobby Charlton and Roger Hunt that stopped my international progress.'

From Arsenal it was on to Nottingham Forest in February 1966. Forest were in the relegation dog-fight, and without Baker's goals they would surely have sampled Second Division football. He became known as 'Zigger-Zagger' by an adoring Trentside public.

The remarkable influence that Baker could have on a team was superbly displayed in the next season as Forest raced to a wholly unexpected second-spot finish in the League. In fact it was only the Manchester United side of Best, Charlton and Law that foiled Forest in their unlikely title bid.

In 118 matches for Nottingham Forest, Baker scored 41 times. It was a return that was envied by several clubs, and one of them – Sunderland – secured his services in June 1969 for a £30,000 transfer fee. The club once known as 'the Bank of England side' were still not averse to buying big names in a desperate bid to reclaim the glory days.

Sadly, Baker felt that his time with the 'sleeping giants' of Sunderland was wasted.

'I didn't really enjoy my time on Wearside. The then manager, Allan

Brown, played a very defensive system which left me quite exposed up front. Looking back I had a choice of Stoke City or Sunderland, and given my friendship with Gordon Banks I maybe should have picked Stoke.'

Yet Baker was immensely popular with the Roker Park faithful. His dashing direct style and natural ability around goal appealed to a support that had been brought up on a diet of fine strikers. That said much for the patience of the Sunderland fans for Baker's arrival coincided with a horrible spell. The club quickly slipped to the foot of the table, and he didn't score until the dying days of December (in a 1–1 draw with Manchester United), one of only two goals he scored that term. Relegation swiftly followed, and although he was among the goals in the Second Division campaign that followed he was eager to be out of a club in turmoil. When his chance came it was from a most unexpected quarter.

On a winter's morning in January 1971 Hibernian fans awoke to wonderful news. Screaming headlines on the back pages of their morning papers proclaimed that Joe Baker was back at Hibs. Hibernian chairman Tom Hart, ever astute in the transfer market, brought Baker back to Edinburgh. Sure, the great man had by this time endured some indifferent seasons, but he was a mature player who would not only galvanise the support but lend experience and know-how to manager Dave Ewing's younger players.

Certainly Hibs needed something special. Season 1970–71 was slipping into the plain awful category. Baker made his second debut on 16 January against an Aberdeen side that had won an amazing 15 League matches back-to-back and set a British record of 12 matches without conceding a goal. Hibs, however, had failed to win any of their previous eight League games. Moreover they had failed to score in five of them. In a stunning debut Baker scored in a surprise 2–1 win with a classic header.

'The club made me captain for the day, and I can remember running out and realising that I was back home and over 23,000 people had turned up.

I had been away for a decade and knew that I couldn't be as good again, but I did score with a header which won the day.'

It was the return of a favourite son, but times had changed. The trademark pace that had made Baker such a lethal striker was gone and a few pounds had been added to the lithe frame. Yet he retained that Midas touch. He scored eight goals in 11 games, ended the season as the club's top scorer and undoubtedly helped Hibs avoid the drop. The irony is that so much of Baker's career seemed to be spent helping clubs avoid relegation when his talents should have been spent landing silverware.

Baker hung around for the 1971–72 season, but by this stage new Hibs boss Eddie Turnbull was rebuilding his side, and Baker played only 11 games in a League campaign that saw Hibs finish a highly-credible fourth. It was time to move on, and a short trip over the Forth Estuary to Kirkcaldy and Raith Rovers was to be the final move in his senior career.

Dropping down the Leagues did the trick for Baker. He played 24 League matches for Rovers in the 1972–73 campaign and scored an impressive 25 goals, including a five-goal romp against Berwick Rangers. The next campaign brought the curtain down on his playing days, but there was a lovely finale when Hibs drew Raith Rovers in the League Cup. On 12 September 1973 Baker scored his last senior goal at Easter Road.

With his playing days over, Baker dabbled in management. His first experience came in the junior ranks with Fauldhouse United, and then he stepped into the senior frame with Albion Rovers. But in two spells with the down-at-heel Lanarkshire club, he was unable to work any miracles.

Greater success came in the hospitality suites of Easter Road, where Baker charmed an adoring public. And it wasn't just at Hibs that he remained immensely popular, he was welcomed back to Arsenal and Nottingham Forest with increasing frequency as his unassuming manner charmed fans both young and old. He was even invited back to Torino, where supporters remembered him with such passion that he and his wife Sonia were mobbed by enthusiastic fans.

A lovely man to chat with and a friend to many, there was great sadness when he died of a heart attack in Wishaw aged just 63 on 6 October 2003. Almost typically of a man who was exceedingly generous, he was playing a charity golf event at the time. A minute's silence was observed before Hibs home League match against Livingston on 18 October and a special commemorative programme was produced. Hibs even invited many of Baker's former teammates back to Easter Road, and they took an emotional bow on the field before the game. Friends, colleagues and fans gathered from afar for one last time as Hibs said farewell to one of its favourite sons.

JOE BAKER factfile

Born: Woolton, Liverpool, 17 July 1940
Position: Centre-forward
Playing career: Hibernian, Torino, Arsenal, Nottingham Forest, Sunderland, Hibernian, Raith Rovers

Hibs League career:

Season	Games	Goals
1957–58	25	14
1958–59	26	25
1959–60	33	42
1960–61	33	21
1970–71	11	8
1971–72	11	4
Total	139	114

International caps:
One Scotland Schoolboy cap
England Under-23: 6 games (1 while at Arsenal), 4 goals
England: 8 games (3 while at Arsenal), 4 goals

BAKER'S HIBERNIAN GOALS

158 goals in all competitions against the following clubs:

16 – Third Lanark

14 – Airdrie

11 – Kilmarnock

10 – Clyde, Motherwell, Aberdeen

 9 – Peebles Rovers

 6 – St Mirren, Partick Thistle, Falkirk, Hearts, Raith Rovers

 5 – Celtic, Dunfermline Athletic, Dundee, Arbroath

 4 – Queen of the South, Stirling Albion

 3 – Queen's Park, Barcelona, AS Roma

 2 – Dundee United, Ayr United, Rangers, East Stirling

 1 – Hamilton, Morton, St Johnstone

Biggest single haul – 9 v Peebles Rovers

Baker scored against 26 Scottish clubs

PAT STANTON

Just how good a player Pat Stanton was can be gauged by the fact that he won Scotland's Player of the Year award in 1970. It is extremely rare for a non-Old Firm player to scoop the honour, and for Stanton to do so with a club that seldom troubles the honours board says much for his personal qualities. A player of great fluidity, he had a style, drive and single-minded determination that made him popular well beyond Easter Road. He was known as 'the quiet man', but his modest demeanour hid a very driven interior. And it was this blend of qualities that made him such a special player. Only Arthur Duncan was able to make more Hibs appearances than Stanton.

Patrick Gordon Stanton was a pupil of Holy Cross Academy and was destined to be a Hibernian player from an early age. His great grandfather had been a founding father of Hibs, and Stanton continued that fine tradition by becoming a leading figure at Easter Road.

However, his route to Hibs from Holy Cross was anything but straight forward. When playing youth football with Salveson BC he was spotted by Dunfermline Athletic, and their manager Jock Stein gave him a trial and tried to sign him. Had things worked out differently, he could have been a Fife star. But fate intervened, and Pat Stanton joined the only club he ever loved and became a name synonymous with Hibernian.

Serious football for Stanton began with the Edinburgh youth institution of Salveson Boys Club. Scouts from several clubs would watch Salveson in the hope of unearthing a gem, and in 1961 Hibs made him a provisional signing. As was the tradition in the early 60s, they farmed him out to a local junior club to toughen him up, and it was Bonnyrigg Rose who had the task of nurturing the young player.

Here was a gifted player, nicely balanced, who linked powerful, surging runs with a deeply intelligent understanding of the game. He did well with

Bonnyrigg and helped them reach the semi-finals of the Junior Cup before being called up by Hibs. By October 1963 he was a full-time player at Easter Road, and he scored on his debut at Motherwell (albeit in a 3–4 defeat). He never looked back and strolled through a Hibernian career that brought almost 700 appearances.

Six times Stanton represented Hibs in major domestic Cup Finals, and amazingly each and every time he found himself up against Jock Stein's all-conquering Celtic side. This, of course, made landing silverware increasingly difficult. But in 1972 he led Hibernian to their first major Cup triumph in 100 years. And it is entirely right to say that he led them to the win, for he did much more than captain that side.

Quite simply, Stanton inspired Hibs to their 1972 League Cup Final win. Scoring one goal would in itself have been a major contribution, but he doubled his worth by providing the cross for Jimmy O'Rourke to grab the other. It was the first time Hibs had landed a trophy in Glasgow, and Stanton was justifiably proud of his role in that success. On the day, Hibernian crushed Celtic with such ruthless efficiency that there were many inside Hampden Park in complete agreement with Stanton's assertion that the 2–1 result was flattering to the beaten Glasgow club.

'Fans often ask me about my goal, but the funny thing is that these games flash by and you can struggle to recall the details. I think my goal came at a free-kick. I remember nipping behind the Celtic defence and Alex Edwards lifting a pass over their wall straight to me. I got on the end of it and it was in; it was great to score in a Cup Final, but even before that goal I was positive we would do well as we were playing with great confidence.

'I had a hand in the second goal too. I remember getting clear down the right-hand side and anyone who saw me play will know that the right-wing was unchartered territory for me. I looked up and saw someone on the back post, but Jimmy O'Rourke was on the front post, and I went for the easier pass. Luckily for me Jimmy put it away

'Walking up the Hampden steps to collect the Cup was brilliant. I was aware that not many Hibs captains have had that pleasure. Looking back,

it was the one occasion on which we really did ourselves justice. We were a good team, but too often we let the fans and ourselves down. Here at last we had proved that we were capable of beating Celtic.'

There were other highly satisfactory moments, many of them on the European stage. In thrashing the mighty Sporting Lisbon at Easter Road 6–1 in the Cup-winners' Cup, Hibs genuinely scaled the heights. For Stanton the foundations for that super win came in Portugal when Hibs, bedecked in their seldom-used purple away strips, restricted the Portuguese to a 2–1 win.

'I thought we played some of our finest European football that night. We were under pressure for long spells but played as a solid team and worked up an ideal position for the return leg in Edinburgh.'

Only slightly less emphatic than the 6–1 win over Sporting Lisbon was a 5–0 victory over Napoli at Easter Road in November 1967. Hibs had lost 4–1 in Naples and few gave them any hope in the second leg in Edinburgh. But, against all the odds, Hibs won 5–0 and in so doing put five goals past the Italian national 'keeper Dino Zoff.

'I scored one that evening. It was great to beat a 'keeper of Dino Zoff's reputation, and there can't be too many occasions in which Zoff conceded five goals in a game. It was a magical night.'

And of course Turnbull's Tornadoes (as that side was nicknamed) racked up a never-to-be-forgotten 7–0 win at Hearts on New Year's Day 1973. Derby matches are the true 'touchstone' for the bulk of a club's supporters, and nothing is sweeter than emphatic triumph and local bragging rights. Pat never failed to recognise the importance of these games. In the November 1975 derby match at Tynecastle, Hibs trailed to a Ralph Callachan goal until deep into injury time when Pat headed home a corner as Hibs piled on the pressure. It was the archetypal captain's contribution on the ultimate local stage.

A 1967 Hibernian team picture taken before a key Scottish Cup tie. Back row: John Madsen, Joe Davis, Pat Stanton, Thomson Allan, Eric Stevenson, Bobby Duncan. Front row: Jim Scott, Allan McGraw, Pat Quinn, Colin Stein, Peter Cormack, Jim O'Rourke.

But Lady Luck by and large deserted Stanton on the big occasions. In his six Cup Final appearances, Hibs won the League Cup and two Drybrough Cups but fell in the more prestigious Scottish Cup in 1972. Moreover, the defeat was spectacularly painful. In the 1972 Final Dixie Deans scored a hat-trick for Celtic as they romped home 6–1, and in the 1974 League Cup Final the same player repeated the feat in a 6–3 rout. While Stanton was bitterly unhappy that day, spare a thought for poor Joe Harper, the diminutive striker grabbing a hat-trick for Hibs, only to end up clutching a losers' medal.

'Once again we made so many chances but spurned the bulk of them. Having said that, Joe, of course, scored a hat-trick and still ended up with a losers' badge. Nine goals in a Cup Final is pretty unusual, and I can't really remember what wee Joe said after the game. In truth, I think he was as gutted as the rest of us and only long after the event could he take any pleasure from the achievement. He certainly did all that could be asked of him. The other contrast that I remember between this Final and the 1972 match is the weather. It was dark and cold when we won at Hampden in '72, but in '74 it was a glorious sunny day.'

The 1969 League Cup Final also saw Hibs concede six (this time in a 6–2 reversal), so in three major Finals Hibs shipped an astonishing 18 goals.

'I have to say, hand on heart, that the 1969 game could have ended up about 6–5 or 6–6. Believe it or not, Hibs were making chances all through the game. Problem was, we missed most of them. Sometimes people point out that the original Final was postponed due to a bad fire in the main stand at Hampden and wonder if the delay worked in Celtic's favour. However, I honestly don't think it did. Really, on the day, we simply lost a lot of daft goals, but all the same we could have scored the same amount that we lost. I don't remember much about the goals by Eric Stevenson and Jimmy O'Rourke, but I think we were well out of the game by the time they scored. Bob Shankly was our manager at the time, and he was bitterly disappointed.'

But Pat Stanton had little to question himself about in these games, nor indeed in any of his Finals. In the 1972 Drybrough Cup triumph he scored in the quarter-final win over Montrose and repeated the feat in the semi-final humiliation of Rangers. In the Final, Hibs held their nerve thanks largely to the promptings of Stanton and drive of manager Turnbull, Hibs having led 3–0 then been clawed back to 3–3 and endured an extra half hour before running out 5–3 winners.

Several matches of this era can be looked back on as classics. In 1971 Joe Baker returned to Hibs after his sojourns to Italy and England, and that occasion made a huge impression on Stanton.

'We had some big games with Aberdeen around that time, and one that sticks out in my mind was at Easter Road in January 1971. Bobby Clark, that great Aberdeen 'keeper, had not lost a goal for a dozen games or so. Joe Baker had come back to Easter Road, and I scored the first, which ended Bobby's run, and then Joe scored the second and we clinched a 2–1 win. That is definitely a game of fond memories for me.

'Not long after that I scored another goal against Bobby, but it was an own-goal for Scotland... so I don't recall that one quite so often!'

It could also be said that Stanton was unlucky in his international career. In all he earned 16 Scotland caps during his 14-years at Hibs. The first of those came against the Netherlands at Hampden in 1966, but Scotland froze and were soundly beaten 0–3. He wouldn't pull on the dark blue again until 1969, and even then the Scots surprisingly failed to beat Northern Ireland at Hampden. Competing with the likes of John Greig, Billy Bremner and Bobby Murdoch for a half-back spot was a big ask, and it says all you need to know about Stanton's qualities that he managed to gather such a sizable cap collection. But there were defeats by Belgium, Austria, Portugal, Denmark and the USSR as Scotland staggered through a particularly lean patch. What's more, the game that all Scots long to play in – the clash against the Auld Enemy – eluded him.

Stanton collected seven caps for the Scottish League, and in this arena he did achieve the goal of playing against England. Three times he tackled the English on this stage. His first League cap came against England in March 1966 at Newcastle's St James' Park. Scotland won 3–1, and Joe McBride, who scored twice, would later be a Hibs teammate for Stanton. A similar thing would happen against the Irish League a few years later when he got a first-hand experience of the lethal finishing of Joe Harper.

Stanton was a great player and was tremendously respectful of those around him. He was the ideal captain for Eddie Turnbull's side, coaxing and leading in a purposeful way that contrasted well with Turnbull's more acerbic approach. When I came to compile the match programme, there was no better contact for a balanced view on a former colleague or indeed an opponent. On one occasion I asked him who were the best players he had played against, and he responded in glowing terms about his fellow professionals.

'Jim Baxter was a marvellous player. His comeback after breaking his leg in Vienna was against Hibs in a Cup tie, and he was awesome for someone just coming back. Jimmy Millar was a good player for Rangers too. When you think of Celtic it is tempting to name Dalglish, Auld, Hay or Murdoch, but I always thought Willie Wallace, whom I had faced as a Hearts player too, was excellent. Jim Smith of Aberdeen and Andy Gray of Dundee United were others who always impressed. It says a lot for Hibs that we won quite frequently against some of these teams.'

One triumph that Stanton did enjoy has almost been lost in the mists of time. In April 1964 Hibs landed the Summer Cup, defeating Aberdeen in a replayed Final. The Final was delayed considerably by an outbreak of Typhus in Aberdeen that made travelling to the Granite City unwise. It was the first Cup Hibs had landed since winning the same competition in 1941. Perhaps it was fitting for Stanton that the trophy was landed at Pittodrie, for it was a venue he clearly enjoyed.

'I always enjoyed playing at Pittodrie for some reason. Certainly the Old Firm stadiums [Ibrox and Parkhead] and Tynecastle were good to play at, but Aberdeen was always a favourite of mine.'

By the early 70s Stanton was at the peak of his powers and a worthy Hibernian captain. He could organise, he could take responsibility and he could

Stanton is pictured here in typically forceful mode.

dictate the course of a match. In the 1971–72 season he scored nine goals as Hibs surged from mid-table anonymity to a fourth-place finish, and Stanton scored in the Scottish Cup semi-final replay win over Rangers. It was a feat that impressed the renowned English sportswriter Brian Glanville, who noted:

'Undeterred by the fact that Rangers had just eliminated Bayern Munich from the European Cup-winners' Cup, Hibernian held them to a draw, then deservedly beat them. A superb game in midfield by Pat Stanton was at the root of their victory, while Rangers, incoherent on the day, badly missed his injured equivalent John Greig. Hibs might have been ahead by half time, such was their superiority. Stanton in fact gave them the lead with a deflected shot.'

He was even more impressive the following term and not only in the League Cup triumph. Hibs finished third in the League, and with eight goals Stanton had played his role, but ever the modest man he was keen to praise others.

'I was fortunate to play in two really good sides. It was often overlooked that we had a smashing side in the mid-1960s when Jock Stein was our boss. We had quality throughout the team and in Neil Martin, Eric Stevenson, Willie Hamilton and John McNamee had some truly quality and inspirational performers. Of course, the Eddie Turnbull side was marvellous too. John Brownlie, Arthur Duncan, John Blackley, Alex Edwards and Jimmy O'Rourke were all smashing players. I was lucky, therefore, to be at the club when they had two great sides.'

The 1973–74 season had Hibs finishing runners up in the League to Celtic and bowing out of the UEFA Cup to Leeds. Sadly that defeat came in a penalty shoot-out, and it was Stanton who had the nightmare of missing the only kick. As he trotted back to the centre circle, teammates noted his comment 'That's me finished with penalties'. Ironically enough, a few days earlier he had converted a penalty against Clyde.

Never a noted goalscorer, he had netted 26 in three seasons and chipped in with his share of Cup goals. From season 1971–72 he missed only five League games over four seasons. Indeed with 399 League games, 103 League Cup ties and a grand total of 680 matches, Stanton was always one of the first names on the Hibernian team sheet.

Sadly, in early September 1976 he moved to Celtic as a player who clearly had a lot to offer. Poor Jackie McNamara made the journey in the opposite direction, oblivious to the fact that Hibs' favourite player was moving out in the same deal. It says much for McNamara that he overcame such a desperate start to become a great Hibs favourite in his own right. Stanton, meanwhile, had bowed out in an emphatic 9–2 Easter Road victory over St Johnstone.

He was a player whom Celtic boss Jock Stein knew well. Having failed to sign him for Dunfermline, he found himself managing Stanton when briefly manager at Hibs. Now, thanks to the financial power of Celtic, he had him at the centre of his team. With his class and vision, Stanton was a great addition to a good Celtic side, and the 1976–77 season saw him back at Hampden Park for a Scottish Cup Final against Rangers. This time he tasted victory, Celtic edging out their great Glasgow rivals 1–0. Given that Celtic had won the League a few weeks earlier, it was a marvellous case of belated reward for a distinguished career. What was ironic was the fact that Celtic clinched their League title at, of all places, Easter Road.

Stanton was one of only two ever presents in that double-winning Celtic team (the other was Danny McGrain) and that was testimony to his superb fitness. Alas, just when he seemed set to establish himself in Celtic's history an injury picked up in August 1977 against Dundee United effectively ended his playing career. Thus, he was able to make only 37 League outings for Celtic, a far cry indeed from the 399 he made in Hibs colours.

In April 1978 he was given a testimonial match by Hibs, with Celtic appropriately providing the opposition. At that time only Gordon Smith and Lawrie Reilly had been granted such an accolade in the post-war era. The fixture provided an ideal opportunity for a whole host of people to say thank you. Eddie Turnbull, in the match programme, didn't pass up the chance and said:

'Pat Stanton's record of nearly 700 games for Hibs speaks for itself. He will go down in the books as one of the club's finest and longest-serving players.... As a midfield player, he showed class and aggression, and the triangle he helped to form with John Brownlie and Alex Edwards was one of the most exciting features in Scottish football in the early 70s.'

A few months later Stanton bowed to the inevitable and looked to continue his career off the field. He achieved this very quickly with a little help from Aberdeen boss Alex Ferguson, who appointed him as his assistant. As with many things in life, it was a chance encounter that evolved into something significant.

'I had gone to Tynecastle to watch Aberdeen play Hearts and got talking to Stan Smith, who had connections at Pittodrie. Shortly afterwards Alex Ferguson phoned me up and arranged to meet me in Edinburgh. When we met, he offered me the job of assistant manager. I had known Alex for a few years through meeting at SFA coaching courses in Largs. I have to say I always got on well with him and thoroughly enjoyed my time with him at Aberdeen.'

As a Rangers and Falkirk player, Ferguson had come up against Stanton several times, and he clearly admired his qualities. Stanton, for his part, showed his own shrewd realisation of the popularity of footballers as he became the owner of Cairns Bar in Edinburgh's Abbeyhill.

The Aberdeen post took him through to January 1980, and a few months later he landed his first job on his own as manager of Cowdenbeath. The Blue Brazil, as the little Fife club have come to be known, have developed a fondness for former Hibernian employees, and both John Blackley and John Brownlie have managed the club too.

Stanton enjoyed his brief stint at Cowdenbeath, and brief it was. Dunfermline are traditionally the largest club in Fife, and as their fortunes wavered they looked on with interest at Stanton's impact along the road. The 1980–81 season didn't open well for Dunfermline, and in December of

Pat Stanton in the late 1990s was a regular visitor to Easter Road and a star of the hospitality suites.

1980 manager Harry Melrose resigned. The Pars Board of Directors turned to 36-year-old Stanton to resurrect their fortunes, but in his first three games they failed to score and lost each and every match 0–1.

Fate, by this time, was 'having a laugh' and pitched Dunfermline up against Hibs in the Scottish Cup. Over 6,000 saw the Fifers draw 1–1 at Easter Road, and Stanton received a heroes welcome. Two and a half thousand were added to that gate for a reply in Fife that went Hibs way 2–1, but the battle to keep Dunfermline in the middle League was now fully occupying him. As Hibs romped to the title (for they were in the First Division too), Dunfermline bit and clawed their way to survival in a campaign that tested the nerves of the most committed Pars fans.

For season 1981–82 Stanton was determined to see improvement and called upon his old teammate George Stewart to lend some much-needed coaching expertise. He also signed a youngster called Norrie McCathie, who would become a Dunfermline legend. But after a promising start the season fizzled out, and the 1982–83 campaign would be make or break for Stanton at Dunfermline. But by September 1982 he was packing his bags and heading over the Forth Road Bridge for Easter Road. Bertie Auld had resigned and there was no doubt whom the Hibernian boardroom wanted to see in the hot seat. Pat Stanton was back and with enough managerial experience to suggest he would be an asset to the club.

Some Edinburgh football followers swear by the dictum of 'Once a Hibee, always a Hibee', and so it proved with Stanton. Even his nickname 'Niddrie' revealed that he was a man proud of his roots and extremely loyal (Niddrie being one of Edinburgh's outlying districts where he was raised). He took his duties at Easter Road very seriously. So seriously in fact that he resigned in April 1983, frustrated by his apparent lack of progress, only to be reinstated three days later.

'Actually I did enjoy being Hibs manager, although on reflection it was perhaps the wrong time to be in charge of the club. Looking back, I would say the club was undergoing a tremendous period of transition, but I was aware that the chance might never have come along again, and I was desperate to take it when offered. The one aspect I certainly did enjoy was seeing a crop of good youngsters coming through, of whom John Collins, Michael Weir and Gordon Hunter were outstanding examples.'

But 1982–83 was not a classic season for Hibs. With the exception of an 8–1 win over Kilmarnock, Hibs rarely hit the heights and an early Cup exit to Aberdeen effectively ended the season as early as January. The following season was to be significant in that youngsters began to make the first-team grade, but a reliance on youth couldn't bring satisfactory results.

On 1 September 1984 Hibs went down 4–1 at Aberdeen, and Stanton was beginning to feel the strain. He was sent to the stand by the referee, having argued vehemently against an offside decision. A fortnight later he had decided he had had enough of managerial life and once more resigned. Only the presence of poor Dumbarton and Morton sides enabled Hibs to survive, that and the presence of another Hibs legend... John Blackley as the new boss.

Stanton's legacy at Easter Road is immense. As a player he remains one of the most popular ever. Beyond being a super performer, he has a warm and engaging personality. As a manager, he had dignity in adversity and a genuine belief in the value of young players. Today he remains one of the best loved hospitality hosts at the club and his reputation as one of the all-time greats is guaranteed. As he himself put it:

'Oh, I am still a devoted Hibee after all these years. I see all of the home games and my fair share of the away matches too. Working with the Former Players' Club keeps me in touch with all my former colleagues and brings me into regular contact with the fans, and we share some wonderful memories together. Like everyone, I get excited at the start of each season and think perhaps this could be our year!'

Pat Stanton gave Hibernian supporters many excellent years and super entertainment. Quite a legacy for the grandson of a founding father.

PAT STANTON factfile

Born: Edinburgh, 13 September 1944
Position: Half back
Playing career: Hibernian, Celtic

Hibs League career:

Season	Games	Goals
1963–64	15	1
1964–65	33	0
1965–66	34	2
1966–67	33	1
1967–68	26	0
1968–69	33	1
1969–70	31	6
1970–71	30	3
1971–72	32	9
1972–73	33	8
1973–74	32	9
1974–75	34	6
1975–76	33	5
Total	399	51

International caps:
Scotland Under-21: 1 game
Scotland Under-23: 3 games
Scottish League: 6 games
Scotland: 16 games

STANTON'S HIBERNIAN CUP FINALS

1968–69 League Cup v Celtic, lost 2–6
Allan, Shevlane, Davis, Stanton, Madsen, Blackley,
Marinello, Quinn, Cormack, O'Rourke, Stevenson

1971–72 Scottish Cup v Celtic, lost 1–6
Herriott, Brownlie, Schaedler, Stanton, Black, Blackley,
Edwards, Hazel, Gordon, O'Rourke, Duncan (Auld)

1972–73 Drybrough Cup v Celtic, won 5–3
Herriot, Brownlie, Schaedler, Stanton, Black, Blackley,
Hamilton (O'Rourke), Hazel, Gordon, Cropley, Duncan

1972–73 League Cup v Celtic, won 2–1
Herriott, Brownlie, Schaedler, Stanton, Black, Blackley,
Edwards (Smith), O'Rourke, Gordon, Cropley, Duncan

1973–74 Drybrough Cup v Celtic, won 1–0
McArthur, Bremner, Schaedler, Stanton, Black, Blackley,
Edwards, Higgins, Gordon, Munro (Cropley), Duncan

1974–75 League Cup v Celtic, lost 3–6
McArthur, Brownlie (Smith), Bremner, Stanton, Spalding, Blackley;
Edwards, Cropley, Harper, Munro, Duncan (Murray)

JOHN BLACKLEY

Nicknamed 'Sloop' after the Beach Boys hit *Sloop John B*, Blackley was a wonderfully composed defender who served the club both as a player and a manager. In two spells at Hibernian he made over 300 appearances, and as an international he represented Scotland at the 1974 World Cup Finals.

John Henderson Blackley was born at West Quarter near Falkirk in May 1948 and joined Hibs in 1964 from Gairdoch United juveniles when he was just 16. It was something of a coup to persuade the 5ft 10in precociously talented youngster to pledge his future to Easter Road. As Blackley recalled, he had other offers on the table.

'When I was with Gairdoch, a few clubs came along to watch me, and I had offers of trials with the likes of Burnley, Chelsea, Dunfermline and Hibs. I might very well have joined Dunfermline, but a meeting I was due to have with them was cancelled (they were playing in a Cup Final), and it was Bob Shankly of Hibernian who was first to offer me something concrete. I could have waited but was anxious at that time to get something permanent.'

His apprenticeship was a lengthy one, and he did not make his debut until the 1967–68 season. As was typical of that era, Hibs nurtured their young talent carefully, farming the youngster out to junior club Bo'ness. Blackley, for his part, wasn't happy at Bo'ness and was both relieved and surprised when Hibs quickly recalled him to Easter Road with a view to continuing his education in the reserves.

He settled well to the second string side and made his first-team bow against Dundee in the 1967–68 season. Few present that day would have guessed that they were witnessing the start of a lengthy career. But the omens were good from around 1970, by which time Blackley was playing for Scotland at Under-23 level.

Managers came and went at Easter Road, and Willie MacFarlane and Dave Ewing occupied the manager's office before former Hibernian star Eddie Turnbull was drafted in from Aberdeen. Arguably, this was the turning point for Blackley as he was given greater responsibility under Turnbull. Economical with his energy, his style was languid yet studied. He represented the Scottish League against their English counterparts and on the domestic scene partnered former Airdrie centre-half Jim Black. This would be the rock upon which Hibs would build their defence.

By autumn 1972 Blackley would be celebrating a League Cup triumph: Hibs first major Cup win since 1902. Yet he had been to Hampden Finals before with Hibs and usually ended on the losing side; in 1968 it was a League Cup thrashing to Jock Stein's all-conquering Celtic side. If the 6–2 scoreline was a humiliation then how would the crushing disappointment of the 1972 Scottish Cup Final hammering be summed up? Inspired by Dixie Deans, who scored three times, Celtic romped home by a barely credible 6–1.

But Turnbull, the zealous Hibs boss, and Blackley learned their lessons well. In the Dryburgh Cup of 1972, a summer curtain-raiser to the season, Hibs defeated their hooped nemesis from Glasgow 5–3. And it was a triumph built on resolve. Leading 3–0, Hibs seemed to be cruising until a pitch invasion by irate Celtic fans halted the game. When it restarted, Celtic seemed revived, Hibs nervous, and in a flash it was 3–3. Extra-time followed, but fortunately Hibs recovered their composure sufficiently to win 5–3. It was a win at Hampden against the mighty Celtic and would lay the foundations for the League Cup Final a few months later.

The 1972 League Cup triumph was a poignant and significant win for the Hibees. Captain Pat Stanton and Jim O'Rourke had the glory of being the marksmen, but Blackley could derive great satisfaction from shackling the ever dangerous Kenny Dalglish, Lou Macari and Harry Hood. For Hibs the game signalled a golden spell that reached its peak when Hearts were destroyed 7–0 in the 1973 New Year derby match.

John Blackley came back to Hibernian in the mid-1980s. Here he is a little heavier than as a youngster but contemplating a career in coaching.

The match was played at Tynecastle, and Hibs were battling Celtic for the League title. The match programme noted that Hearts had 36 wins to Hibs' 35 in League games at Tynecastle. That record was about to be levelled. Jim O'Rourke, Alan Gordon and Arthur Duncan were all on target as the first half took on the lustre of a dream. Alex Cropley and Duncan added further goals, and amazingly the half-time score was Hearts 0, Hibernian 5.

That in itself would have been a major shock, but Hibs refused to let up and O'Rourke added a sixth. Then, with time running out, Alan Gordon's header hit both posts before crossing the line. Hibs had won the derby in a fashion that would spawn songs down through the decades.

Alastair Alexander covered the game for BBC Scotland, and he saw the match as one of the truly great Hibernian performances.

'That for me was the day that Turnbull's side really clicked. Everything Hibs did came off, and they gave a quite superb performance. I remember during the game saying "Hibs look as if they could score at any time they wish"... three passes later they did. You have to say there wasn't the same intensity surrounding the fixture as there is now. There was a definite sporting side to the game, and Hearts took their beating on the chin. But that 7–0 game was a wonderful football spectacle. The performance of Alan Gordon still sticks out, but it was only part of a great team effort.'

The reward for this exceptional season was a tilt at Europe, and although Blackley, by this time, was well used to the stage, he reckons that Hibs gave their best showings in the 1973–74 Cup-winners' Cup.

'My favourite memory is of playing Sporting Lisbon as Portuguese football was always highly thought of. Over in Lisbon in our very first attack Alex Cropley hit both posts, and although the ball came out it really quietened the crowd and made them respect us. They beat us 2–1 that night, but we turned it round in Edinburgh. European nights at Easter Road were always dramatic, mysterious, laden with excitement, and it was certainly special when we beat them 6–1 in the return leg.'

In March 1972 Blackley was capped by the Scottish League against England at Middlesbrough's Ayresome Park. His good friend John Brownlie was also in a strong Scotland side that lost a thrilling match 2–3. This was a prelude to gaining seven full caps, and as Scotland only conceded four goals in those matches Blackley can be said to have had a significant input.

At the end of the 1973–74 season Scotland played in the World Cup Finals in West Germany. Managed by former Hibee Willie Ormond, he included 24-year-old Blackley in his travelling squad, and, having helped Scotland beat England 2–0 at Hampden in the weeks running up the Finals, he had earned his spot. Thus, in the very first match he lined up against the unknown African side Zaire. In three matches Scotland were unbeaten, and they became the first team ever to exit a World Cup without having lost a game. For Blackley the tournament had mixed properties.

'One of the highlights of my career was getting into the Scotland team and playing against Zaire in the World Cup Finals in 1974. But the Zaire game was very nerve-wracking, and until that match I used to think I could handle any amount of football tension. I thought I played all right, but I was dropped for the next game and quite cut up about it at the time.'

Things were not always sweetness and light for Blackley at Hibs either. Three times he featured in Hibs matches that were abandoned, and one really riled him as it almost seemed to confirm the belief that the Old Firm were favoured by bizarre decisions from Scottish football officials. In October 1974 a table-top clash with Celtic was halted in dense fog with fully 83 minutes having been played. This proved controversial in the extreme, and more than one sports journalist at the time wondered if the same decision would have been made were Celtic leading. With just seven minutes left, Hibs were winning at fortress Parkhead 2–0 and proving their title credentials in emphatic fashion. The replayed match was drawn.

By 1975 it was Jock Wallace's Rangers, rather than Jock Stein's Celtic, that were thwarting Hibs ambitions. Blackley was by then a highly-experienced professional, pitting his wits against the Rangers players on the domestic scene and in the battle for international caps. There was an unusual outcome in the key League clash at Ibrox in the summer of 1975. Both sides were desperate to make a good start to the season, and, in a 1–1 draw at Rangers, Blackley and his great rival Derek Johnstone both scored, but incredibly both were own-goals.

Worse, and more surprising, than either the Celtic abandonment or own-goal distress, was the infamous 1977 Scottish Cup exit to little Arbroath. Having salvaged a 1–1 draw at Gayfield Park, John Blackley cancelling out Tommy Yule's strike for the minnows, Hibs went into the replay firm favourites to qualify for the quarter-finals. In a disastrous showing the club were bundled out 1–2, and perhaps the seeds were sown for the end of the Turnbull years.

By 1977 the Turnbull era was showing signs of having peaked, and Hibs were financially pressed. Blackley was by this stage playing as a sweeper where his slight lack of pace was not a major hindrance. Newcastle United had long admired 'Sloop' and twice seen bids for the elegant defender rejected. Now the timing was ideal, and when the Magpies boss Richard

Dinnis offered a cheque for £110,000 Hibs could not refuse. At the age of 29, arguably his peak, Blackley was pitched into the English game.

It was a dreadful time to join Newcastle. The Tynesiders were a huge club, but they were struggling to live up to their reputation. Despite winning their first game of the season, they had then proceeded to lose the next eight, and Blackley was chipped in against Derby County with a restless crowd making everyone extremely nervous. United lost and would end the season relegated, having used a staggering 35 players.

Bill McGarry took over from Dinnis and promptly headed back to Easter Road to add John Brownlie to his squad. Even reuniting Blackley with his long-time friend did not work any miracles, and United failed to gain instant promotion, but for Blackley there was at least the personal satisfaction of winning the Newcastle United Player of the Year award.

It was a time when Newcastle dabbled with some frequency in the Scottish market, and they had tried to lure Paul Sturrock of Dundee United in the months before Blackley's move. Ironically Sturrock and Blackley would work together in football but not at that particular point.

'When I was 31 Newcastle freed me and former Manchester United and England legend Nobby Stiles took me to Preston North End, although I did have an offer to join Hearts. It was tempting to think I could come back to Edinburgh, but given my Hibernian background I couldn't have seen my presence at Tynecastle working out. Preston, like Burnley and Blackburn, had been a great Lancashire club and there was a deal of history about the place, what's more it was a very happy family club. I really liked playing there but was out on my ear when Tommy Docherty arrived with his 'brand' of man-management skills.'

Joining Preston in July 1979, he played there for just under two seasons and made over 50 League appearances for the famous old club. Blackley had

John Blackley learned a great deal from several managers, but perhaps not the inimitable Tommy Docherty.

mixed feelings when in only his second match for North End he helped them beat Newcastle 1–0. Punching above their weight, Preston secured a mid-table finish.

When his spell in England was over, he returned to Scottish football with Hamilton Academical, then playing in the Scottish First Division. The role saw John pitched in as a player-coach, assisting boss Dave McParland, and passing on his undoubted experience to Hamilton's young team. Fulfilling his role with considerable drive, it was no surprise when Blackley succeeded McParland into the managerial chair in October 1982.

It worked well, and Accies went from strength to strength. Others noticed their progress, and Pat Stanton, struggling a little to establish himself as Hibs boss, invited Blackley to be his assistant. Thus, in the autumn of 1983 John Blackley was back at Easter Road.

Initially it was meant to be a player-coach role, and Blackley was called into action on the field fairly quickly. He made his second debut for Hibs on 8 October 1983 away to Rangers, but he was only able to make 16 outings and missed several matches through injury. Sadly, he had to concede that his body, while eager, was ageing.

'I was delighted to be back at Easter Road, and it was in a player-coach role. However, my hamstring was going, and eventually I had to hang up my boots rather than let everyone down.'

Hibs avoided relegation, but only because Motherwell and St Johnstone were so poor. The Scottish Cup ended in the traditional ignominy when little East Fife won 2–0 at Easter Road in a replay, and the scant consolation was that Hibs got a first-hand view of the Fifers' young striker Gordon Durie and noted his name.

The 1984–85 season opened up with Hibernian in terrible form, winning only one of their opening six League games and bowing out of the League Cup embarrassingly to Edinburgh's third club – Meadowbank Thistle. Long-suffering fans were growing restless and attendances were plummeting. Things had to change.

The defeat against Dumbarton on 15 September was too much for Pat Stanton to bear, and he resigned soon afterwards. Rather conventionally, John Blackley was persuaded to stand in as interim boss and made such a good job of things that Hibs elected to give him the job on a permanent basis. He quickly added the aforementioned Gordon Durie of East Fife to the squad, and Hibs gradually clawed their way to safety at the expense of Morton and Dumbarton.

Blackley seized the opportunity he had been given with heart-warming enthusiasm. Hibs got off to a mixed start in 1985–86 but with youngsters Collins, Hunter and Kane all maturing nicely the side began to show promise. However, inconsistency plagued the club, which lost the opening six League games of the season then remained unbeaten in the next 10!

Intermingled with these League matches were League Cup ties, and Hibs rose to the Cup occasion. Cowdenbeath were beaten 6–0 with a hat-trick by Steve Cowan, then Motherwell were thrashed 6–1 with a hat-trick by Gordon Durie. Many thought that Celtic in the quarter-finals would be a hurdle too far, but a 4–4 draw preceded a penalty shoot-out win for Hibs.

In the semi-finals Rangers lay in wait and were hot favourites, but Blackley pulled off a master stroke in buying Gordon Chisholm shortly before the game, and he and Durie scored in a first-leg 2–0 win. A 1–0 reversal at Ibrox in the second leg was not enough to prevent Hibs marching to a Final meeting with Aberdeen in October 1985. Unfortunately, Alex Ferguson's team proved too strong on the day. Their goalkeeper Jim Leighton, who had not conceded a single goal in the competition, maintained that sound record.

Blackley, however, set himself high, arguably unrealistic, goals, and although he seemed to be turning the club around he was not happy with his own perception of progress. His was the insecurity common in fledgling managers striving to escape from a previous identity as a popular and successful player.

'On reflection I was probably too young at the time. If I had my time again I would have avoided the post and gone elsewhere and learned from someone for a few years more. I really regret it now because I always wanted to be boss of Hibs, and sadly I felt I failed when I actually had the chance.'

In 1986–87, however, things did not go according to plan, and this despite an incredible opening game to the season when Hibs turned over Rangers in a game that saw the Ibrox club's new player-manager Graeme Souness sensationally sent off after an infamous tackle on George McCluskey. Sadly, Hibs came down to earth very quickly, and the good result was undone by failing to win any of their next eight Premier League matches. As Paul Kane, one of the band of youngsters impressing on regular basis, noted:

'John maybe wasn't ready to be manager, but he gave it his best go, and in bringing Tommy Craig to the club he gave the younger players at Easter Road a wonderful grounding in the game. We did well in the Cups with John, but were too inconsistent in the League.'

Indeed, a run of only three wins in 17 League starts saw 'Sloop' tender his resignation in November, and he dropped out of the game for a little while. Having left Hibs, it could have been the end of his footballing career. Fortunately he was friendly with the chairman of little Fife club Cowdenbeath and was invited to take over as manager at Central Park. It was a move that restored Blackley's failing confidence and enthusiasm in football. He caught the eye at long-neglected Cowdenbeath and was soon happy to tackle a bigger task.

'When Dundee appointed Englishman Dave Smith as their boss, he looked for someone with local knowledge to assist him as he settled in to Scottish football. I was delighted when he invited me to be his assistant, and it was an opportunity I was keen to take.'

Sadly, Dundee were relegated, and Blackley was out of a job again before becoming a community coach at Falkirk. That let him see how Jim Jefferies

and Billy Brown worked at Brockville. Given the success they would enjoy at Falkirk, Hearts and Kilmarnock, they clearly had good knowledge to pass on, and Blackley was a willing recipient.

By now it was clear that not only did Blackley like coaching but that he had impressed the wider Scottish football community with his commitment and perseverance. Out of the blue he received a call from St Johnstone boss Paul Sturrock. The former Dundee United striker was boss of Saints from August 1993 to September 1998, and John Blackley became a key figure by his side. When Sturrock was asked to take over at Dundee United he naturally took Blackley with him to Tannadice.

Here he saw at close quarters the stress levels that modern football management can induce. While going through a particularly bad spell, United boss Sturrock collapsed pitch-side during a tense League game. The need to establish an appropriate work-life balance was never better illustrated. Sturrock finally escaped the fierce hot-house atmosphere of Scotland's Premier League by taking the long road south to join Plymouth Argyle in sleepy Devon.

Surprisingly, this move to a rural haven proved to be a forward move, and Argyle flourished under Sturrock's guidance, and right by his side was John Blackley. When Sturrock was enticed to Southampton, it was Blackley who held the helm at Plymouth briefly, but the two were reunited at firstly Southampton and then by 2005 at Sheffield Wednesday.

A classy player and a diligent manager, John Blackley had made the most of the chance he was offered when playing with Gairdoch in the 1960s. Only 11 players made more appearances for Hibernian, and in becoming club manager he became only the sixth post-war Hibee to both play for and manage the Edinburgh club.

JOHN BLACKLEY factfile

Born: Falkirk, 12 May 1948
Position: Central-defender
Playing career: Hibernian, Newcastle United, Preston North End, Hamilton Academical, Hibernian

Hibs League career:

Season	Games	Goals
1967–68	3	0
1968–69	13	0
1969–70	31	0
1970–71	29	2
1971–72	33	2
1972–73	29	0
1973–74	31	1
1974–75	22	0
1975–76	34	1
1976–77	31	0
1977–78	7	0
1983–84	16	0
Total	279	6

International caps:
Scottish League: 1 game
Scotland Under-23: 4 games
Scotland: 7 games

BLACKLEY'S GOALSCORING RECORD

John Blackley was not a noted goalscorer for Hibernian. Defensive duties dominated his game, but just occasionally he would venture forward. When I asked him about his goalscoring, he said 'I don't remember scoring too many, but I know I had quite a few own-goals!'

1970–71 ... penalty in a 2–2 home draw with Cowdenbeath
1970–71 ... scores at Kilmarnock in a 4–1 defeat
1971–72 ... scores in a 2–2 draw at Airdrie
1971–72 ... scores the only goal in a 1–0 home win over Morton
1972–73 ... final goal in Hibs 3–1 League Cup win at Queen of the South
1973–74 ... Pat Stanton hits a hat-trick and John a single in a 5–0 romp against Clyde at Easter Road
1975–76 ... a pulsating match against Aberdeen at Easter Road ends with a corner to Hibs. In a crazy goalmouth scramble, 'Sloop' knocks the ball home from a mere six inches

NEIL MARTIN

Neil Martin was one of the best British centre-forwards of the 1960s. It was his misfortune to serve a series of average clubs rather than to have a chance to shine on the bigger stage his talents deserved. Yet, in his short Hibernian career he made an impact that few can forget. Seldom has a player looked so invincible in the air or so powerful on the ground.

The golden rule for a centre-forward is to score and score again. Neil Martin did that with style. He played 65 League games for Hibs and banged in an amazing 53 goals. With 100 goals in the Scottish League by the time he left for England, he wasted no time in repeating that feat south of the border. The key component of his game was his lethal heading ability. He could engineer chances from the slightest of openings, peeling off his marker to earn the room to allow him to bullet home stinging headers.

Martin began his career with Tranent Juniors in East Lothian. This was the traditional route into professional football for so many youngsters at the time. He lived in Tranent, a small mining town, and viewed his home club as the natural testing ground. Here was a local opportunity to find out if he was good enough to consider trying to make a living from football. Clearly he was, as he was spotted there by Alloa Athletic, a struggling League side, and scored 23 goals in just 48 matches for them.

'I was 18 when I joined Alloa Athletic in 1959 from Tranent Juniors. It was one of those lucky moves and very much a case of being in the right place at the right time. The local policeman in Tranent was also a scout for Alloa, and he had seen me playing [he was actually a cousin of the famous John White of Scotland and Tottenham]. He convinced me to move to Alloa, and it was a great move for me. Mind you, it wasn't without its problems. I didn't have a car and so to get the 50 miles from Tranent to

Alloa was an awkward journey involving several buses. Eventually I got to know a few of the lads at Alloa who lived in Broxburn, and I would travel over to Uphall and get a lift with them.'

His two seasons in the Second Division had many clubs considering his talents, and given Alloa's perilous financial position they were duty bound to accept the first notable offer they received. He stayed with the Second Division side until 1961 when George Farm (a former Hibernian

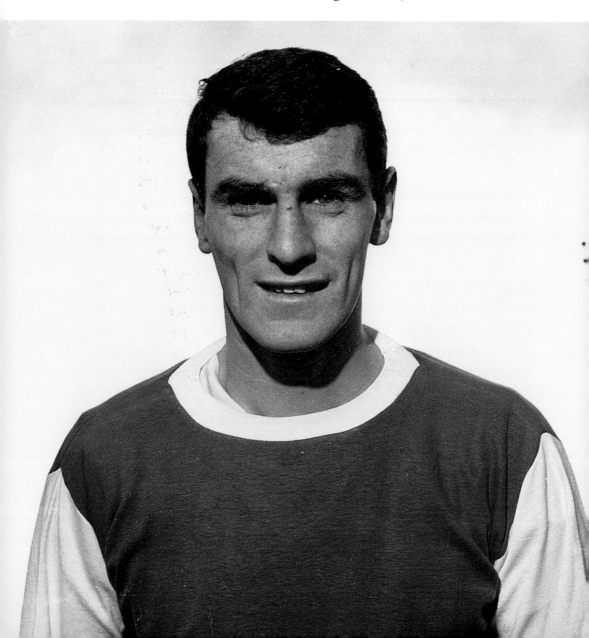

goalkeeper) signed him for Queen of the South. It was a huge sum for the Dumfries club but £2,000 very well spent.

'I was with Alloa for about a year and a half when Queen of the South boss George Farm persuaded me to move to Dumfries. That was in November 1961, and they had a good team at the time and were making a real push for promotion. As well as me, they signed Willie McLean [brother of Jim and Tommy who would star as managers] and they had Ivor Broadis in their team too. We got promotion and the move really saw my career take off. However, I must have been keen for, looking back, it was another epic travelling situation. I didn't sell up in Tranent and move to Dumfries, rather I would stay in digs and come home whenever I could. Looking back, my wife was very understanding for we were only just married!'

Martin had two seasons with the Doonhamers and was seldom far from the goalscoring routine. The Dumfries club won promotion in 1962, and in 1963 they stayed up against all the odds. He became something of a talisman at Palmerston Park, scoring 33 goals in 61 League matches. The 'clincher' for Hibs came in the 1962–63 campaign as the Hibees avoided relegation by a mere two points. Raith and Clyde went down, while Hibs and Queen of the South stayed up. The latter had relied heavily on the goals of Neil Martin.

Hibs, and in particular boss Walter Galbraith, sensing a very special talent, stepped in and snatched him up to Edinburgh for £7,500. It was a move that pleased his wife in particular.

'It was a strange move in that it was actually initiated by a *Daily Record* reporter – Alex Young. Alex used to pop into the chemist shop where my wife worked and eventually asked my wife why she kept going on about Queen of the South. She explained that her husband played for them, and Alex asked if I would be interested in joining Hibs! Soon afterwards Walter Galbraith got in touch, and I was delighted to join.'

The July 1963 transfer heralded the start of an exciting era for Martin and for Hibs. He made his debut in the League Cup at St Mirren and scored the Hibs goal in a 1–1 draw. Four days later he opened his Easter Road account against Dundee United, and in the section of six matches he scored five goals, thus helping Hibs reach the quarter-finals. He was less prolific in early League games but did score in a 3–4 defeat at Motherwell, a match that saw a debut goal for a youngster called Pat Stanton.

But three days later Hibs failed to beat little Morton in a drawn League Cup semi-final despite a goal by Martin, and a week later they sensationally crashed out of the competition to the Greenock club. In what would be a bitter irony, the Morton goal was scored by Allan McGraw, a player Hibs long coveted but failed to land until 1966.

Back in the League, Neil Martin began to find his feet, and the matches against his former club Queen of the South summed up the season. In the first game in Dumfries, Hibs lost 3–2 despite a brace from him. It was all change at Easter Road in March when Hibs romped home 5–2 and Martin banged in four goals. Soon it would be all change in the Hibs manager's office too as Walter Galbraith left and was replaced by Jock Stein.

With 20 goals from 28 League games, Martin had more or less paid his fee, but when Hibs landed the Summer Cup he had truly arrived, and he gave Stein the perfect honeymoon present. A hat-trick against Falkirk and three goals in the two-leg semi-final showed his value. Hibs won the Cup by beating Aberdeen in a replayed Final, a match that was delayed due to the outbreak of Typhus in Aberdeen.

Capped by the Scottish League, Neil Martin had made the most of his switch to full-time football. Physically uncompromising and the owner of a great shot, he was a leader in every sense of the footballing requirement. On 18 March 1964 he had pulled on the Scotland jersey for an inter-League fixture with England at Roker Park, Sunderland. Scotland drew 2–2, and he further enhanced his reputation by grabbing a goal. That goal would prove significant later in his career.

Media coverage focused understandably on Martin's prodigious leaps and powerful headers, but there was much more to his game. He could hold the ball with confidence and was adept at bringing those around him into the game. He was also exceptionally brave, breaking both his nose and his wrist in that first season at Easter Road.

Martin had 78 Scottish League goals going into the 1964–65 campaign and earned another League cap when he played in Dublin against the League of Ireland. But the domestic game was proving his 'bread and butter', and when he scored the third goal of his hat-trick against Celtic in March he had hit the century. It was a season in which Hibs supporters increasingly realised that their club would struggle to hang on to their prolific striker.

The loss of manager Stein to Celtic did have a destabilising effect and had hurt Hibs. Thus, Martin rated his hat-trick at Parkhead among his finest moments in green:

'Two memories stand out for me when I look back on my time at Hibs. Beating Real Madrid 2–0 in a friendly when they had a really good team was quite something. I think we were the first Scottish team to beat them, and I remember Puskas was still part and parcel of the Madrid set up at that time. Another happy day came when I scored a hat-trick in a 4–2 victory at Celtic Park in March 1965. It was all the sweeter because Jock Stein was their manager and had left Hibs to join Celtic just a few months earlier. I still believe we would have won the double had Jock not left for Celtic. We were going great guns – in the semi-finals of the Scottish Cup and lying second in the League – when Jock moved to Parkhead. It was a bitter blow from which we never fully recovered.'

1964–65 had seen Hibs terrorise both halves of the Glasgow divide. In just 31 matches Martin scored 25 times, and as well as his trio at Celtic there was the notable feat of helping to beat Rangers three times. An early season 4–2 League win at Ibrox was quite unexpected, but by the time Rangers were beaten in January in a League match at Easter Road the team were flying and confidence was high.

There were over 44,000 at Easter Road for that eagerly awaited game, and Martin rose to the occasion. It was his towering header that won the day and gave Hibs their first League double over the Ibrox club since 1903. That 1–0 win was only marginally less pleasing than the marvellous 2–1 Scottish Cup win at Easter Road. But it was typical of Hibernian in this era that yet another semi-final ended in defeat. This time Dunfermline edged home at Tynecastle Park... so often a Scottish Cup graveyard for Hibs. Hibs had a side brimming with courage, but there was 'an achilles heel' and it seemed to be big Cup ties. The Famous Five had struggled in Cup semi-finals and so too did countless Hibs sides after them.

Having lost in a League Cup and then a Scottish Cup semi-final in consecutive seasons, as well as landing the Summer Cup, Hibs clearly had a good side. They proved this in the 1965 League Cup campaign, their first without Jock Stein at the helm. His replacement Bob Shankly needed money to fund new signings but relied heavily on the goals of Neil Martin. Simultaneously, Martin was keen to have his pay reviewed by the Easter Road management, and Hibs were tempted to sell him to fund new buys.

Such background machinations did not impinge on the player's drive. Despite losing their opening game to Falkirk, they won their group in a canter. In the quarter-final Martin's old club Alloa provided the opposition, and a remarkable second leg saw Hibs shatter their opponents 11–2. Martin extended no sympathy to his former teammates, grabbing four of the 11 goals. This set up a last-four clash with Celtic.

In the semi-final many expected stronger, wealthier Celtic to win, but Martin scored twice at Ibrox in a pulsating 2–2 draw. Unfortunately, but quite predictably, the replay went against Hibs as Celtic ran out 4–0 winners. The reason wasn't just Hibs' awful big-match record, but the fact that Martin had been transferred in between matches. His last game in the green of Hibs came on 9 October, and he scored in a 2–2 home draw with Motherwell.

'My move out of Hibs came about when I asked for a rise and couldn't reach a compromise with Hibs. I knew about Sunderland, having played for the Scottish League down there, and scored a late equaliser in a 2–2 draw.

When they expressed an interest I was hardly going to turn them down. The fans were fanatical, and I knew it was a great footballing town, but the sheer passion actually surprised me.'

Martin was sold to First Division Sunderland in October 1965 for £45,000, a considerable profit on Hibs' initial £7,500 outlay. His departure was the second high-profile exit from Leith to Sunderland, with full-back John Parke having made the same move in November 1964 for £33,000. But the attractions in going to Wearside were obvious. Sunderland manager Ian McColl was building a veritable Scottish colony, and Martin was joining the likes of Jim Baxter, George Mullhall and George Herd at Roker Park.

The best way for a forward to make an impact is to score on his debut and Martin duly obliged. His goal at Sheffield Wednesday could not prevent Sunderland losing 3–1, but seven days later he scored the opening goal in a 3–0 Roker Park win over Northampton Town. He proved an instant hit on Wearside, and his input was vital in helping Sunderland pull away from the threat of relegation.

Neil Martin had scored over 100 goals in Scottish football before he arrived at Roker Park. Soon he was rampaging towards the magical ton in

English football. In his second season at Sunderland he scored 20 League goals and six in an exciting FA Cup run. Hat-tricks against Blackpool and Peterborough United were the obvious highlights. But he also played in both 3–0 derby wins over Newcastle United in what was a highly-satisfying season for the Rokerites. The match against Peterborough saw Sunderland win by a staggering 7–1, and Martin faced an old friend.

Martin shortly after joining Sunderland.

'The thing I recall about the Peterborough game is meeting up with Johnny Byrne, who had been at Easter Road too. He was worried about the match beforehand and jokingly asked me to "take it easy" on them. But unluckily for him Sunderland had had a bit of fright in the previous round so really went into the Peterborough game with a sound attitude. All seven goals were scored by Scots: quite a feat!'

Having too many red-blooded Scots in the same Sunderland team was not a guarantee of success. This was evident when one club bowed out of the Cup after an epic clash with Leeds that needed three games to split the teams. The replay at Elland Road gave Leeds their record home attendance. When the tie ended it was amid Scottish controversy.

'As well as facing a very good Leeds team, we felt we were up against the match officials too. They gave Leeds the softest of soft penalties in the final minute of the last game. We were incensed and surrounded the referee to complain. George Herd and George Mulhall overdid it and were both sent off, and we crashed out of the Cup in high controversy. I can tell you that we cheered Chelsea on when they beat Leeds in the Final that year.'

The season had been a personal triumph for Martin. He had missed only one match all season, and he played for Scotland in their epic World Cup qualifier against Italy. A last-minute goal by Rangers' John Greig sent Hampden Park into a frenzy, and Martin would look back on that match as the most incredible atmosphere he ever played in.

'That was a fantastic match, with around 117,000 crammed into Hampden. Jim Baxter, who was also at Sunderland, played that night, and it was he who slipped in the pass that gave John Greig his crack at goal. To beat a team like Italy, so famous for their resolute defending, was really satisfying.'

The following domestic campaign saw Martin unsettled, and although he scored 10 goals he left the club in February after an away match at Sheffield Wednesday. Thus, with a neat touch of symmetry his Sunderland career both began and ended with matches at Hillsborough.

'It is true that I did score a lot of goals for Sunderland, but I still think that had I not picked up a bad back injury I would have scored more. I spent a fair bit of time on the treatment table and that stopped me in my tracks. It took me quite a long time to get back to top form after that injury. Again I was in a good team, and I was probably signed as cover for Brian Clough, the regular number nine. However, he was struggling to get over a knee injury, and he never made it back, and the first home game I played in for Sunderland was in Brian Clough's testimonial match against Newcastle United. We had some great derby clashes with Newcastle, and I really loved those matches. The fans were fanatical but not in a really nasty way, and the banter from the crowd was good.'

If relegation had been a constant spectre while at Sunderland, then much the same happened when he joined Coventry for £90,000 in February 1968. Sunderland had doubled their money and that was good business in any book. But he proved his worth to Coventry by netting 18 goals in the final 15 games of the season, which undoubtedly kept City in the top flight. The following season his prolific goalscoring made him the top scorer for City.

'Sunderland had sacked manager Ian McCall and that made me determined to leave Wearside. It was luck that Coventry came in and were such a good club. They were struggling a bit when I joined them, but I scored a glut of goals and we stayed up. They had a reputation for being a bit of a family-run outfit, and we gradually built a good atmosphere and strong little club. They got into the Fairs Cities Cup when I was there (the forerunner of the UEFA Cup) and achieved their highest ever League finish. Eventually they asked me if I fancied a move to Nottingham Forest! When a club says a thing like that to you, you know that you no longer feature in their plans.'

In February 1971, having scored 40 goals in 106 Coventry matches, he moved to Matt Gillies's Nottingham Forest, and it was here that he would enjoy his longest spell with any club. Defiantly optimistic that he could provide the goals needed, he fitted in well. He made 119 outings for Forest and scored 28 goals. But his loyalty and perseverance came at a price, as it was with Forest that he first tasted relegation in his career.

'My move to Forest was a big one in that I was 31 years old at the time, and yet they were still spending £75,000. I had five good years there, and, by the time I was leaving, players like John Robertson, Martin O'Neill and Tony Woodcock were breaking through. Brian Clough actually inherited the nucleus of a very good side, but he worked wonders with it. I met up with former Hibee Peter Cormack at Forest, which was really good, and we remained firm friends thereafter.'

By July 1975 his career as a player was beginning to near its end and taking him ever further south. He was sold to Brighton & Hove Albion, but he managed only 17 outings with them (mind you, it brought eight goals) before he joined Crystal Palace. He followed that with a brief spell in Ireland at St Patrick's Athletic, then Dave Mackay, who had played with distinction for Hearts, offered him a job coaching at Walsall. But more exotic climes lay just around the corner.

'I had been reserve-team coach at Walsall when the great Hearts, Tottenham and Scotland legend Dave Mackay was boss there. Dave was well-known in the game and seldom without offers of some kind. When he got the job of managing the Kuwait national side, he asked if I wanted to go out with him. The deal was fantastic so I gave it a go. Thank goodness I did as I ended up staying for eight years and had a further one in Dubai.'

When he returned to Britain, Martin found it hard to break back into the game and settled into life in Sutton Coldfield in the English midlands.

Scottish Daily Express team pictures were a feature of the summer newspapers in Scotland. This version shows Hibs lined up for the start of the 1964–65 season, and Martin is third from the left in the middle row.

He owned a couple of pubs in the area before upping sticks and returning to Scotland and Tranent.

Throughout his career Neil Martin was recognised as an accomplished striker, but few Hibs fans probably realised just what an excellent return he achieved in a goals-to-games ratio. He, along with Joe Baker, has the best goal average of any Hibernian player. A return of 0.81 goals per game is quite remarkable.

Looking back, he had a career that offered excitement for those watching and a touch of the exotic for Martin himself. The sight of him flying through the air to bullet home another header was one of the highlights of the mid-1960s at Easter Road. His Hibernian career may have been short and sweet, but it lingered in the memory long afterwards. It may be many years before Hibernian has a striker who can rattle in 53 goals in just 65 matches.

NEIL MARTIN factfile

Born: Tranent, 20 October 1940

Position: Centre-forward

Playing career: Alloa Athletic, Queen of the South, Hibernian, Sunderland, Coventry City, Nottingham Forest, Brighton & Hove Albion, Crystal Palace, St Patrick's Athletic

Hibs League career:

Season	Games	Goals
1963–64	28	20
1964–65	31	25
1965–66	6	8
Total	65	53

International caps:

Scotland Under-23: 1 game

Scottish League: 2 games

Scotland: 3 games

MARTIN'S HAT-TRICKS

7 March 1964 (home) v Queen of the South (4 goals)

20 May 1964 (home) v Falkirk

14 November 1964 (home) v Third Lanark

2 January 1965 (home) v Falkirk (4 goals)

22 March 1965 (away) v Celtic

22 September 1965 (home) v Alloa (4 goals)

25 September 1965 (home) v Falkirk (4 goals)

ARTHUR DUNCAN

When a player earns the nickname 'Nijinski' then one of his qualities is glaringly obvious. Nijinski had been the first racehorse in 35 years to win the Triple Crown of the St Ledger, the Derby and the 2000 Guineas and was the fastest horse in the world in the early 1970s. Arthur Duncan was the quickest winger Hibs had enjoyed for years and the nickname followed.

But Duncan was more than just quick, he was extremely fit. So fit that in his Hibernian career, which extended from 1969 to 1984, he established the record number of appearances for the club, clocking up a superb 448 League matches. What's more, he was good enough to go from being a Scotland left-winger to a quality left-back without any loss of contribution.

Duncan was born in Falkirk in 1947 and was an outstanding football prospect while at Falkirk High School. By a quirk of geography, at that time Falkirk schools were playing in the Glasgow League, and this helped him secure a spot in the Glasgow Schools side against their London counterparts. The real spin-off for him was that the scouts for Glasgow's senior clubs attended these games, and Partick Thistle were so impressed with what they saw that they instantly offered the youngster terms.

Arguably, it was Thistle who were actually the lucky party. When he was only 14, Duncan had been invited to train with Liverpool, and he spent school holidays travelling to Merseyside with a view to having an apprenticeship at Anfield. Fortunately Jags boss at the time, the former Rangers legend Willie Thornton, saw enough in the 16-year-old to persuade him to join Thistle.

'I had no doubts about joining Partick. I had visited Liverpool for three consecutive summers and was training with Liverpool at other times too.

However, Partick made me so very welcome that I instantly felt the club was the right one for me.'

Willie Thornton had been a dynamic centre-forward for the Glasgow giants, scoring 188 goals in just 303 League fixtures, and had relied hugely on the excellent service his wing partner Willie Waddell supplied. Thus, he was ideally placed to know a good winger when he saw one. He was also a firm believer in the system of farming youngsters out to junior clubs and promptly sent Duncan off to Gairdoch United. Duncan would meet another boy at Gairdoch – John Blackley – and in time they would become key components of the Hibernian side.

Duncan's first-team debut for Partick has entered Maryhill folklore.

'I remember my debut as it came against Alex Hamilton of Dundee. Hamilton was famous at the time for talking players off their game. He used to carry a complimentary ticket and would hand it to young opponents and say "Here son take this and sit in the stand; you'll not get a kick of the ball today anyway".'

Thistle proved to be a good club for Duncan. An interesting blend of youth and experience, they provided a solid platform for a youngster learning his trade. He developed sufficiently to earn a Scotland Under-17 cap in Kosovo and then found himself capped by the Scottish League. The first of a collection that would ultimately grow to four League caps came in September 1967 at Belfast's Windsor Park against the Irish League. And it is worth recalling the line up as it included two men who would eventually be Duncan's teammates – Hibs' Peter Cormack and Pat Stanton.

McCloy (Motherwell), Wilson (Dundee), Provan (Rangers), Stanton (Hibernian), McKinnon and Greig (both Rangers), McLean (Kilmarnock), Penman, Ferguson (both Rangers), Cormack (Hibernian), Duncan (Partick Thistle)

Duncan had made his Thistle debut in the 1965–66 season and scored an impressive nine goals in only 15 outings. By the time 1969 was fizzling out, he was a fixture in the Partick team having made 117 appearances and bagged 33 goals.

Soon events in the east of Scotland were about to impact directly on Duncan's career. In 1969 Hibernian fans were raving about an outrageously talented left-winger by the name of Peter Marinello. A George Best lookalike, Marinello was a teenage sensation, and when Arsenal lured him to England in January 1970 there was real despondency at Easter Road. The £100,000 cheque was a huge amount for a teenager, but many supporters reckoned that 'the new George Best' was irreplaceable.

How wrong they were. For a third of the fee Arsenal had paid, Hibs went out in December 1970 and bought the winger who would become an institution at Easter Road. Willie McFarlane had been a keen fan of Arthur Duncan and was delighted to lure the youngster from Firhill. Fortune

An athletic attempt on goal by Arthur Duncan at Celtic Park. On this occasion he is thwarted by Celtic goalkeeper David Latchford. Covering any slip is Johannes Edvaldsson, and watching from a distance is Kenny Dalglish.

favoured Hibs. Duncan himself recalls it was good timing on the Edinburgh club's part.

'I was in dispute with Thistle at one stage, and Sammy Kean, a former Hibs player, was the Thistle assistant manager. He spoke to Hibernian scouts and soon Willie McFarlane, then the Hibs boss, got wind of my discontent in Glasgow. As a boy, I had enjoyed watching Falkirk and Hibs [an uncle was a real Hibee through and through] so on several occasions I had gone along to watch games at Easter Road. So all in all the move to Hibs was a great one for me.'

A cheque for £35,000 was written to prise Duncan out of Maryhill, and that represented a then record fee for Hibs. He complemented a side that could boast talents like Joe McBride, Johnny Graham and Eric Stevenson. Confusingly, he wasn't the only Duncan on the Hibs books at the time; Bobby Duncan was a teammate for a short while, which confused sports writers at the time and can trip up club historians even now.

It is as well to clear up the two Duncans situation at this point. Bobby, who was an able full-back, joined Hibs in 1963 from Bonnyrigg Rose and stayed until 1971 when he took the road to East Fife. There were only seven League games left for Bobby, who was two years Arthur's senior, as a Hibs player when Arthur arrived, but their presence on the staff at the same time did confuse some.

Signed by McFarlane, Duncan had to survive a managerial jitter that saw McFarlane replaced by Dave Ewing and then decisively Eddie Turnbull. Regardless of the uncertainty in the background, Duncan's impact was almost instant in a Fairs Cup tie against Liverpool at Easter Road. Hibs lost 0–1 when the towering Welsh striker John Toshack grabbed the only goal of the game, but Duncan, too, had scored, only to see his goal disallowed.

There would nonetheless be plenty of goals in his career. He grabbed 112 as a Hibee and his haul of 73 League goals puts him ahead of such luminaries in Hibs history as Bobby Combe and Eric Stevenson. There were some games where he really went to town, and in October 1971 he turned on the style against his local club Falkirk, grabbing four in a scintillating display.

Duncan was the gifted and athletic expression of Turnbull's side. His galloping forays down the wing added a touch of excitement and raw energy to a side that was disciplined, powerful and well-coached. Hibs fans had always believed that flair was a part of the Hibernian experience, and he did much to continue that tradition.

In February 1971 Hibs met Hearts in a key Scottish Cup tie. There are no bigger games in the local diary, and when Duncan hit the winning goal in the 81st minute his place in Easter Road affections was secure. In a searing run, considering the stage of the game, he ran deep into Hearts territory before unleashing a drive high into the Maroon's net behind Jim Cruickshank.

The early 70s saw Hibs win back-to-back Dryburgh Cups, and when they added the League Cup in the autumn of 1972 they owed much to Duncan's trickery and threat on the wing. His pace would carry him beyond all but the quickest of defenders, and if the cross wasn't on he was more than capable of nipping inside and testing the 'keeper himself. But the sum of Turnbull's side was greater than the parts, and Duncan recognised this.

'The sheer spirit at Easter Road both on and off the field was something special in the early 70s. We had a couple of really, really good seasons. In fact, in the 1972 season, myself, Alan Gordon and Jimmy O'Rourke weren't far off getting a hundred goals for the club.'

Abundant goalscoring was a distinctive part of Hibs' culture in this period. Magnificent as trophy successes were they were, in the local psyche overshadowed by Hibs astonishing 7–0 win at Hearts on New Year's Day 1973. Duncan was a star in that game. Hibs raced into a 5–0 half-time lead, and he scored twice in that captivating 45 minutes. Strikers like Jim O'Rourke and Alan Gordon were able to complete their doubles in the second half, but he had effectively killed off Hearts in a magnificent first-half performance. It is a game worth dwelling on. Duncan himself recalled the match with genuine pride.

'I think it was one of those games where everything we tried came off, and we could probably have scored more than seven that afternoon. To win your local derby 7–0 is unheard of, but to win by that margin on your opponents ground just beggars belief.'

The Hibernian side has entered Easter Road folklore: Herriot, Brownlie, Schaedler; Stanton, Black, Blackley; Edwards, O'Rourke, Gordon, Cropley and Duncan. The goals came thick and fast, but, unlike the 4–1 win Hibs achieved at Tynecastle in 1967, this time they didn't let up. In the 4–1 game Hibs switched off after racing into a 4–0 lead inside the opening 10 minutes. This time they exerted continual pressure. Jimmy O'Rourke opened the scoring in the ninth minute, and then Alan Gordon doubled the advantage on the quarter-hour mark. Just before the half hour, Duncan grabbed his first and then silky Alex Cropley made it 4–0 in the 35th minute. Just two minutes later Duncan scored again, this time with a rare header, and that was the situation by the time Hearts limped off stunned at the interval.

Perhaps inevitably, the second half struggled to match the first. But in the 56th minute the effervescent O'Rourke made it 6–0, and Alan Gordon headed the seventh and final goal with a full 15 minutes left to play. And this was no ordinary Hearts side either. The Maroons had lined up with Garland, Clunie, Jefferies, Thomson, Anderson, Wood, Park, Brown, Ford, Carruthers and Murray. There were well over 1,000 appearances between that Hearts side so they were hardly inexperienced. But on the day it was very much 'men against boys', and Hearts were simply swept aside.

The *Daily Record* had no doubt that Hibs had scaled new heights as 1973 opened and predicted a bright future:

'Can Hibs stay at the top of the League? They took over the leadership yesterday on goal difference from flu-hit Celtic after the 7–0 humiliation of

Hearts at Tynecastle – the widest victory margin between the teams for more than 50 years.

'Although they have played two games more than Celtic, Hibs are in the mood to fight for the title until the last day...and that might be April 28, when the two contenders meet at Easter Road.

'Unstoppable Hibs are the team of the moment – and the team of the future, so full of football, loaded with confidence and talent.'

Alas, Hibs were stoppable, and Celtic proved it. The April clash when it came was nothing like a title-decider as Celtic had won the League by a considerable margin. Indeed, Hibs failed to win any of their last seven League games of the campaign. A season that had promised so much had simply fizzled out, and Hibs didn't even manage to finish second in the League.

Nevertheless, the love affair with goals continued unabated. In 1975 Hibs faced Celtic in a League Cup Final that quickly escalated into a 90-minute shoot-out, with the emphasis firmly on scoring rather than stopping goals. Remarkably, despite a Hibs player scoring a hat-trick, the club lost. It was a veritable goal-fest of a Final, with Celtic winning 6–3.

'We lost despite the fact that Joe Harper scored a hat-trick. Dixie Deans scored a hat-trick for Celtic too, as he frequently did against us. How big Jim Black at centre-back must have hated the sight of Dixie. The scoreline, however, didn't tell the story of the game, and I felt that we matched Celtic for most of the match and were sunk by conceding three goals in quick succession.'

Sadly, losing Hampden Finals was something Duncan became used to. In the 1972 Scottish Cup Final Dixie Deans managed another of his famous trios against Hibs, and the outcome was a 6–1 thrashing that entered the annuls as one of Hibs' darkest days. Duncan, though, did his level best for the Hibs cause.

Before the game, Celtic boss Jock Stein had singled out Duncan as a genuine threat and was right to do so. After McNeill had shot Celtic into the lead it was he who manufactured an equaliser for Hibs. Speeding down the left wing, onto a pass from John Blackley, he sent over a low cross that was just beyond the reach of Celtic 'keeper Evan Williams, and Alan Gordon was able to slide in and poke the ball home. Sadly, it was to be the only moment of joy for Hibs in a thoroughly dreadful showing that perpetuated the myth that Hibs and the Scottish Cup just were not made for each other. Duncan's day had started well but simply fell away, and in the 62nd minute, with the score only 3–1 in Celtic's favour, he was involved in a clash of heads and carried off.

In 1979 the club went back once more to contest a Scottish Cup Final, only to lose a twice-replayed Final to Rangers. Given that Duncan conceded a penalty (which Alex Miller, later to manage Hibs, missed) it was hardly a happy occasion, and it got worse before the evening was over.

Undoubtedly, the most famous Hibernian own-goal of them all was scored by Arthur Duncan in that 1979 Scottish Cup Final second replay. His flashing header, from a Davie Cooper cross, in extra-time decided a Final that had seen two boring 0–0 draws before the final game burst into life with Rangers narrowly winning 3–2. Some indication of how poor the matches were can be gleaned from the dreadfully disappointing attendances. There were just over 30,000 at the second replay, whereas the first game had attracted over 50,000.

Some wonderful stories surround Duncan's own-goal. The best I have heard concerned my good friend Stuart Crowther, whose brother was serving in the army in Germany at the time. Having attended the first two games, he was sickened to be missing the second replay as he was on patrol. However, he had asked colleagues to keep him informed on the progress of the match. Imagine his excitement then when a colleague informed him that 'the game's finished 3–2'.

'Who for?' asked an agitated young Private Crowther, barely able to conceal his excitement.

'I don't know' came the reply, 'but some guy called Arthur Duncan has scored the winner.'

Cue major celebrations for young Private Crowther. Only after a night of joyful excess was the cruel truth revealed. Duncan had indeed scored the winning goal in the Cup Final, but it was an own-goal.

Fortunately, international football was kinder to Duncan. Recognition in the shape of full caps followed in the wake of the success of the Turnbull's Tornadoes side. He made his Scotland debut on Tuesday 13 May 1975 against Portugal, coming on as a late substitute for Tommy Hutchison of Coventry City. Amazingly, by September 1975 he had won the last of his six caps, thus making his Scotland career a real rapid-fire experience. Only one of those games was lost, but as it was 5–1 to England at Wembley in front of 98,000 fans it was a pretty painful experience. Yet it gave Duncan what he considered his most memorable footballing outing.

'That day was the highlight of my career. Unfortunately we lost 5–1, but I will never forget coming out of the tunnel and seeing the mass of Scotland flags. It made the hairs on the back of your neck stand up.'

The Scottish Premier League also started in 1975, and, while Celtic's Bobby Lennox had the first hat-trick, the first Hibs hat-trick in the new-look League was grabbed by Arthur Duncan in a 4–3 victory over St Johnstone in November 1975.

Throughout his career Duncan was adaptable and indeed versatile.

'I played in every position except centre-half for Hibernian. I was even in goal one day, replacing Jim McArthur when he was injured during a game at Ibrox and had to go off. That was a natural thing for me to do for I always fancied myself as a goalkeeper at training and had mucked about in goal for years. However, wide on the wing was my favourite position.'

Just how well Duncan adapted to the changing face of football and his own changing body can be seen by looking at the 1979 Scottish Cup clash with Hearts. Whereas the 1971 derby had seen him as a flying winger, the 1979 match featured him at left-back, proof indeed of his versatility and his dedication to life as an athlete. How ironic then that his Hibernian career should end with an injury. Having said that, it is only fair to acknowledge that it was an unusual injury.

'I broke my collar bone against Meadowbank Thistle in an East of Scotland Shield game. I was usually pretty good at riding tackles, but this time I came to earth with a bump, and as it was a hard surface I came off second best. That injury was significant as it helped end the practice of first-team players playing in the Shield. The injury did not go down well with the Hibernian managerial team, and thereafter the game became a youth or reserve fixture.'

It was hardly surprising that Duncan was awarded a testimonial match. Not only was he loyal, but he was extremely popular on the terraces. An international select provided the opposition on 3 May 1981, and he followed the likes of Lawrie Reilly, Gordon Smith and Pat Stanton in receiving this highest of local accolades. His final League game in a Hibernian shirt came at Easter Road on 7 April 1984 at home to Dundee United, and fittingly Hibs won 1–0. After 14 years as a Hibernian player, he moved on, dropping down to the lower Leagues to continue his love-affair with football.

However, Duncan didn't have far to move to continue his career, barely a mile in fact. Meadowbank Thistle were managed by Terry Christie, who was a good friend of his and was able to convince him to continue in senior football. In the 1984–85 season his name appeared in a different team-sheet, but my goodness it appeared. In a 39-game League campaign he missed only six matches. One game he didn't miss was a third-round League Cup tie against Hibs. How Hibs fans wished he had as astonishingly little Meadowbank ousted the Hibees 2–1 in a huge shock.

Meadowbank were en route to the semi-finals with a side that contained a clutch of useful journeymen players, but they should surely never have beaten a Hibernian team that contained Alan Rough, Gordon Rae, Jackie McNamara and Brian Rice. He was joined by the likes of Graeme Armstrong (who would break the Scottish League appearance record), Tom Hendrie, Peter Godfrey, Adrian Sprott and Alan Lawrence. Only 3,202 bothered to turn up for the tie, and Ralph Callachan's goal couldn't save Hibs from a humiliating reversal.

When he hung up his boots, Duncan worked nine to five for West Lothian NHS as a podiatrist (chiropodist). However, his departure from football was temporary, and eventually he returned to the game in order to work as a part-time physiotherapist for Livingston (the club which Meadowbank had evolved into – moving from Edinburgh to the new town of Livingston in the process). It was only when the West Lothian club turned full-time that he stepped down, but he still popped in on an ad-hoc basis.

Duncan joined Hibernian when pipe-smoking Harold Wilson was in Number 10 Downing Street. By the time he left, Margaret Thatcher was Prime Minister. From beer and sandwiches in Number 10 to Wapping and the miners' dispute, the changes had been immense, and, like the British political landscape, the life and times of Arthur Duncan at Easter Road had certainly seen many alterations.

ARTHUR DUNCAN factfile

Born: Falkirk, 5 December 1947

Position: Outside-left, left-back

Playing career: Partick Thistle, Hibernian, Meadowbank Thistle

Hibs League career:

Season	Games	Goals
1969–70	7	3
1970–71	23	4
1971–72	30	11
1972–73	33	10
1973–74	33	6
1974–75	31	12
1975–76	36	13
1976–77	30	2
1977–78	30	5
1978–79	35	1
1979–80	27	0
1980–81	39	1
1981–82	32	1
1982–83	35	2
1983–84	27	2
Total	448	73

International caps:

One Scotland Schoolboy cap

Scottish League: 4 games

Scotland Under-23: 1 game

Scotland: 6 games

THE TOP 12 HIBERNIAN APPEARANCES

Player	Hibs Career	League appearances	
		Start (subs)	Total
A. Duncan	1969–1984	436 (12)	448
P. Stanton	1963–1976	397 (2)	399
E. Turnbull	1946–1959	349	349
W. Ormond	1946–1961	348	348
G. Rae	1977–1990	337 (11)	348
G. Hunter	1983–1997	333 (6)	339
P. McGinlay	1988–2000	299 (23)	322
A. Sneddon	1980–1992	303 (9)	312
G. Smith	1946–1959	310	310
E. Schaedler	1969–1978 & 1981–85	291 (8)	299
J. Paterson	1948–1959	283	283
J. Blackley	1967–78 & 1983–84	278 (1)	279

FRANCK SAUZÉE

'Sauzée, there's only one Sauzée', rang the popular terrace song at Easter Road in the late 1990s. And seldom had a song been sung with such pride or genuine depth of feeling. Franck Sauzée came from France to Edinburgh in the veteran years of his career and totally won over the Hibernian support. Classy, committed, cultured, he had all the skills of a top international. What's more, he seemed to fall in love with Hibs, and the fans reciprocated.

Even a short-lived and plainly unsuccessful spell as Hibernian manager was unable to remove the gloss from Sauzée's association with Easter Road. Here was a man whom fans and players alike could look up to. For many years to come he will remain one of the all-time favourite Hibees. Perhaps if he had been given more time as a manager he may have enjoyed the same success in that role as he did while a player. But nothing could ever tarnish the memory of a truly exceptional footballer.

Before you can appreciate the impact of Franck Sauzée on Hibernian, it is necessary to paint a comprehensive picture of his pre-Hibernian career. Beyond all doubt, this was Alex McLeish's finest signing as Hibs supremo. While many fans appreciated that Sauzée was a player with an impressive pedigree in the game, few realised that he had scaled such consistent heights while in France.

Franck Gaston Henri Sauzée was born on 26 October 1965 in Aubenas, France. Aubenas lies in the Ardeche region of Eastern France and is a small fishing village. Perhaps it is an unlikely setting to mould an international football star, but Sauzée remained convinced that it was a place that gave him character and strength.

By the time he embarked upon a professional career, Sauzée was 6ft 2in, physically impressive and possessed an amazing will to win. A prodigiously

talented schoolboy, he joined Souchax from school and made his debut for them in an away League match at Rouen on 17 August 1983. He was only 17 but would enjoy a career that eclipsed his age.

That first season brought 19 French League matches and a solitary goal. Eric Cantona was a teammate, and Sochaux became known for their flair. Playing as a midfielder, he quickly displayed the composure and creativity that would serve him well throughout his career, and with his ability to read the game he soon showed sufficient knowledge to play the occasional game as a sweeper. A dedicated trainer, Sauzée believed in the value and importance of good habits to progress. Healthy eating, sensible living and constant practice fast-tracked his career in double-quick time.

Sauzée spent five seasons with Sochaux, the most dramatic of which came in 1986–87 when the club that held great store in its youth system slipped into the Second Division. Showing typical grit and determination, he not only helped them achieve promotion but steered them to the French Cup Final, which they lost rather unluckily 4–5 on penalties to a strong Metz side. He had certainly done his bit, scoring a goal in the semi-final win and converting his penalty in the shoot-out. From the despair of 1987 came the rewards of 1988, but the Cup Final outing and promotion were small-beer compared with being part of the French Under-21 side that won the European Championship.

In the summer of 1988 Sauzée was transferred to Olympique Marseille. Slotted into a big club with ambitions to match, he began to excel. In 1989 Marseille were French champions and Cup winners (receiving the Cup from Président Mitterrand) and 12 months later retained the title. His stint at Marseille was broken by a season with Monaco in 1990–91 (coached by Arsene Wenger) and the honours continued to roll as he collected another French Cup-winners' medal. But it was a solitary season with Monaco, and 12 months after signing he was back with Marseille, and this time history was about to be written.

In 1992 Marseille again won the League, and with it came entry to the European Cup. Remarkably, no French side had ever won the grand old trophy, but with a side that could boast international stars like Sauzée, Boksic,

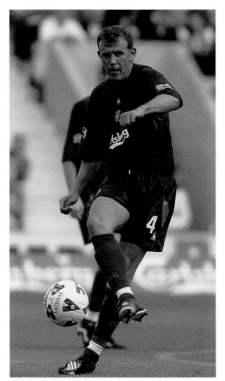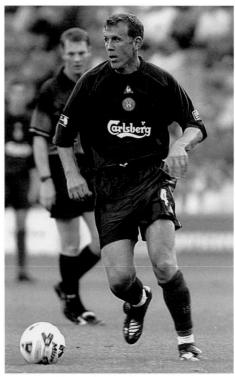

Arriving towards the end of his career, Franck Sauzée made a huge impact at Hibernian.

Voller, Desailly and Deschamps, that was put right. En route to the Final Marseille had to overcome a strong Rangers side, and they did so thanks largely to a 1–1 draw in France when Sauzée's goal thwarted the Glasgow club.

It is a matter of some pride, and an interesting curio, that Franck Sauzée was the first French player to score a goal in the revamped Champions League that we now take for granted. But sadly the Marseille triumph in Munich 1993 was later tarnished when the club owner Bernard Tapie was found to have been involved in serious irregularities, and Marseille were not allowed to defend their trophy. There was further disappointment in 1994 when France failed to reach the World Cup Finals in America, losing by a last-minute goal at home to Bulgaria and with it their place. In a career that brought many highs, it would be fair to say that Sauzée had to learn how to handle the downside of football.

Marseille began to disintegrate almost immediately after their ground-breaking win, and Sauzée moved to Italy to play in Serie A with Atalanta

Bergamo. It was little wonder that coach Francesco Guidolin was desperate to sign him. Not only was he clutching a European Cup medal, but his 12 goals in 35 League matches had made him a key player in what was a star-studded Marseille side.

Unfortunately, the Italian job was not to Sauzée's liking. He spent an unhappy season in Bergamo, the club finished second bottom and were rather easily relegated. His solitary season there brought one goal in 16 starts, and in truth he never settled into the Italian game. So much so that for the start of the 1994–95 season he was back in France, albeit in the colours of the slightly less glamourous RC Strasbourg.

From June 1994 to 1996 home for Sauzée was the French-German border. He was to play 65 League games in his two seasons in Strasbourg and notched nine goals. The club reached the French Cup Final only to fall narrowly to the giants of Paris St Germaine. Nevertheless, entry to the UEFA Cup was secured, and here Sauzée's repertoire of skills had the ideal stage.

Drawn against Tirol in the first round, Sauzée scored in the 1–1 away draw and then bagged two in the 6–1 home demolition. Ujpest Dosza were beaten in the next round, and it took a Roberto Baggio-inspired Milan to end the run, but even then Sauzée grabbed the Strasbourg goal in the cauldron of the San Siro. Perhaps more significantly, he struck up a friendship with the likes of David Zitelli and Freddy Arpinon, which would have a significant benefit for Hibernian further down the line.

From Strasbourg it was back to the south of France with Montpellier. Although his first season there went well (7 goals in 27 matches), his second season was a disaster as a personality clash with the coach confined him to the sidelines. Thus, when Alex McLeish lured Sauzée to Easter Road there was enormous interest. Here was a genuinely sophisticated player with 39 French caps, 9 international goals, a European Cup medal, a clutch of French Championship and Cup-winners' badges and 15 seasons' worth of experience. The question that was on everyone's lips was would he prove a veteran winding down his career or bring a clutch of fabulous talents to Eater Road? Fortunately for Hibs, it was the latter that prevailed.

Alex McLeish was the youngest ever Hibernian manager. A sound player with Aberdeen and Scotland, he had gained all the honours the domestic Scottish game could offer and added a European Cup-winners' Cup and 77 caps to boot. As a Scotland international, he had played against Sauzée in the run up to the 1990 World Cup Finals and marvelled at the athletic Frenchman's skills. Thus, when it became clear in 1998 that he was available for transfer Alex strained every sinew to make the affable Frenchman his key signing.

Sauzée knew little, if anything, of Hibs, but did like Scotland. A keen fisherman, he knew of Scotland's standing when it came to trout and salmon fishing and viewed Edinburgh as an attractive city. A visit to Scotland and a tour of the sights with Alex McLeish was a big part of the job done, but the key was McLeish's unbridled passion and enthusiasm for football. Rapid Vienna and Basle were keen to add him to their staff so McLeish had to be at his most persuasive. Fortunately, having had a coach at Montpellier with whom he could not communicate, he viewed McLeish as a breath of fresh air.

Signed in February 1999, he joined a Hibs side that was roaring towards the First Division Championship. He was 33 at the time and immediately saw the bigger picture.

'When you join a club that is 17 points ahead in the Second Division you know that you have really joined a First Division club. I spoke with Gilles Rousset, the Hearts goalkeeper, and he confirmed that Hibs are a solid club with a good manager. But the decision to come here was mine and mine alone. The reason I am here is because of the attitude and commitment of Alex McLeish.'

It was amid the unlikely and rather unlovely clutter of Falkirk's Brockville Park that Sauzée made his Hibs bow. On a mud-bath of a pitch Hibs won 2–1 with only 10 men and opened up a 20-point lead at the top of the table. In effect, promotion was sealed and Sauzée liked what he saw, and, despite lacking fitness, said:

'I'm very optimistic that I can be a success here, but it will take me some time to make my mark.'

How true those words were to prove. Russell Latapy, the Trinidadian midfielder, suddenly found himself with an equally talented colleague, and the two gave Hibs an edge that few clubs in Scotland could match. But arguably the real benefit of having Sauzée on board was the stature he gave the club. A host of players from France now knew who Hibernian were, and players such as Fabrice Henry, David Zitelli, Freddy Arpinon and Marc Libbra undoubtedly joined Hibs due to the presence of Sauzée.

Promotion was won with 'miles' to spare. Sauzée played in nine First Division games and simply got better in each match. Organising midfield and helping in defence, his ability to 'see the pass' and fire in blistering free-kicks made him stand out. With each passing week a goal got nearer and nearer, and then finally on 24 April at home to Morton he scored the goal his play had merited. With a fitting sense of occasion, he saved his second goal for the last match of the season when, amid a party atmosphere, Hibs beat Falkirk 2–1. Presented with the trophy on the pitch after the game, it was John Hughes who was club captain in name, but Sauzée who was the true king of Easter Road.

The style and power of Franck Sauzée arre perfectly captured in these action shots.

There were few more committed players. In the derby against Hearts at Easter Road in March 2000 Sauzée lost several teeth when scoring a header during a 3–1 win. With the match delicately balanced at 1–1, he got on the end of a Tom Smith cross to arc a lovely header beyond Niemi in the Hearts goal. Unfortunately, his follow through saw his mouth connect with Gary Naismith's head and four teeth were lost.

'For about 20 seconds the pain was so bad that everything around me didn't seem to exist. I was dizzy and didn't know what was happening. Then I heard a loud roar from the crowd, and I thought "Hey, maybe I've scored here". I knew I had when I heard Mixu Paatelainen shouting in my ear "Frankie, you've done it, you've scored!" Suddenly all the pain I was feeling disappeared. It's so special to score a goal in a derby match because I know how much these games mean to the supporters – it's the biggest day of their season.'

By this stage Hibs were pushing towards the Scottish Cup Final. Mixu Paatelainen, another highly-experienced veteran, was crashing in the goals as Hibs adapted well to the top flight. Paatelainen, a mighty Finn in every sense of the word, said of Sauzée:

'Franck is so intelligent in the way he sees passes; he's one of the best players I've played with in terms of vision and passing ability.'

It was a good first season back, and the club reached the Scottish Cup semi-final only to fall unluckily to Aberdeen. On the eve of the match Sauzée committed himself to the club for a further year. His reasoning struck a chord with every fan

'For the last two months the reaction of the Hibs fans to my retirement has been incredible. Whenever I have been into the city centre the fans would come up to me and ask me to stay for one more year. I have also spoken to the players and had the same reaction. When you have a passion, and feel all the people have the same passion, you want to do even better. I never thought it was possible to see people have this reaction with me. It struck me in the heart. I am very happy in Scotland – the last 15 months have been good in my life and in the football.'

Although Hibs lost that semi-final they were back the following year and this time made no mistake. Livingston were pushed aside 3–0, and in the Final against Celtic Hibs ran the Glasgow defence ragged for 15 minutes before slipping to defeat. Arguably, were it not for Russell Latapy going 'off the rails' as the season reached an exciting climax, Hibs might have landed silverware.

The 2001–02 season was to be Sauzée's last in Edinburgh. Before the club got down to the serious business they had a pre-season tour of France and played against his former employers Marseille. It was clear that he was still a legendary figure with the Marseille fans. They mobbed him before and after the game, and he responded with a flamboyant showing sprinkled with typically powerful shooting.

When the season got underway a fortnight later, Sauzée was in good shape and clearly appreciative of the club helping him prepare for a big season. It started brightly enough. Quickly among the goals, he was the club's leading scorer in early September and played in the never-to-be-forgotten UEFA Cup epic against AEK Athens.

'AEK showed how good a side they were, yet few would deny that we did really well against them. I think the only thing we missed was that extra touch of experience, but that will come. The whole UEFA Cup thing was a fantastic journey for the club, and it shows quite clearly the value of doing well in the domestic League. The other big bonus is that matches such as those against AEK improve the players' mental strength. Getting back into Europe is a key stage in progressing as a side.'

But Sauzée played his last game for the club in late October against Dundee. An Achilles injury was proving troublesome, and while he returned to France for treatment things changed rapidly back at Easter Road. Alex

McLeish was persuaded to take over the managerial vacancy at Rangers. The 36-year-old Frenchman was announced to the media as the successor to Alex McLeish at a Friday lunchtime press conference. Hibs, in fairness, recognised his lack of experience and cleverly lined up former Under-21 coach Donald Park as his assistant. Just how seriously Sauzée took the role was made clear at the conference when he announced that he wouldn't be playing again.

'I am very happy and very proud as well to be manager here, I'm not afraid, and I'm delighted to work for the club. I have seen the club improve a lot in the three years since I joined, and I will do my best for Hibs.'

For the Hibs board the 14 December decision must have been easy. There was no way they could have taken the risk of over-looking the fans' favourite. With his wealth of experience, popularity and media charm, he was the candidate from heaven. Had Hibs let him slip through their fingers to succeed elsewhere, they would have been guilty of a catastrophic mistake for which the fans would never have forgiven them.

As it was, he lasted just 69 days. In that period Hibs won a Scottish Cup tie against Stranraer. Eleven League matches had come and gone without a single victory, but most damaging (and surprising) had been a League Cup semi-final defeat to Ayr United.

I had an inkling that not all was well. When I spoke to Sauzée after his return from France, he was surprised that the draw for the Scottish Cup had taken place and asked me who Hibs had got. In an interview for the programme just a few weeks earlier, when I had asked him about absorbing football 24-7, he had been less than convinced.

'I am professional footballer all week, both on the field and in training; therefore, when my job is finished, I want to do other things. I like going to the cinema, and I love fishing. Basically I like to relax away from football; I devote myself totally to it as a job so my spare time has to be completely different. I haven't given any thoughts as to what I might do when I stop playing. I remain a professional footballer, and I am 100 percent focused on playing. For now my concentration is devoted to getting fit again and forcing my way back into the team. For me, thinking about my career after I stop playing is not a problem because I only have an interest in playing for now. Perhaps when I do retire from playing I can think about coaching, but I am not sitting for any tests or qualifications at the moment. Hibernian supporters can rest assured that all of my energies are devoted to playing.'

They were hardly the words of a man who desired management. His period in charge went badly from the off. Game number one was away to Dunfermline, and the early dismissal of Spanish striker Paco Luna meant that Hibs played for the bulk of the game with only 10 men... a 0–1 defeat was the outcome. A 0–0 draw with St Johnstone and then a 0–3 home defeat by Rangers (in which two Hibs players, McManus and Laursen, were sent off) followed. But a difficult November ended with a 1–1 draw at Hearts with club captain John O'Neill grabbing an injury-time equaliser.

But luck was rarely with Sauzée in the dug-out. Dundee United snatched a late winning goal at Easter Road in early January and then Hibs bumbled to a 0–0 draw at Stranraer in the third round of the Cup. Seven days later Freddy Arpinon was sent off for spitting at an opponent in Dundee, and Tom McManus was injured so badly that he wouldn't play again that season. The 0–1 defeat was hardly surprising. A deep crisis of confidence gripped the club now that even a 4–0 home Scottish Cup-replay win over minnows Stranraer couldn't assuage.

Two-nil up against Kilmarnock, the defence was beset by the late panic that had characterised much of the McLeish reign, and Kevin McGowne's last-ditch strike earned Killie a 2–2 draw. Then astonishingly Hibs scored three times at home to Aberdeen and still lost, again conceding a goal in the very final minute. Sauzée snapped and, in a memorable press conference, swore, banged the table and generally revealed just how much such poor form hurt him.

A few days later Rangers gave Hibs a right royal thrashing in a 4–1 Scottish Cup exit, and soon afterwards it was revealed that Ulrik Laursen wouldn't play again that season. Celtic were hardly the ideal opponents to run into, but Hibs surprised perhaps even themselves by drawing 1–1, and in goalscorer Garry O'Connor they had a new star in the making. Jarrko Wiss and Gary Caldwell were lured from English football, and Sauzée seemed to be steadying the ship.

But 6 February was to be D-Day. Hibs were up against Ayr United in the League Cup semi-final. Ayr, a Division below Hibs, were hardly leading lights in their own Division, and all that was required from Hibs was a decent 90 minutes and a place in a national Final would be theirs. What followed was a shocker, with Hibs playing as poorly as they had all season and Ayr eventually winning in extra-time when veteran striker Eddie Annand converted a penalty.

Understandably, Sauzée cut a forlorn figure in the press room after the game.

'I cannot accept how we lost tonight. We have international players in our team, but where were they? We did not deserve to win; we did nothing. In football you must be up for every game. We did well against Celtic and then this! I did not see one player on the pitch.'

In any language it was a blistering attack on players who had lost by missing chances then conceding a very harsh penalty. The mood was hardly helped when Hibs crumbled 0–4 at Motherwell in their next match. But, as former Hibee Dirk Lehmann noted after the game, Hibs had started well and hit the bar before Motherwell scored the first of their second-half goals.

Sauzée was quite correct to note after the game that his players, despite lacking confidence, were a full 11 points ahead of St Johnstone and relegation was highly unlikely. Quitting was never on his mind, but matters were taken out of his hands when the club drew their next fixture 1–1 with Dunfermline. The decision was made to sack the man who clearly loved Hibs and had given them some of their classiest moments in years.

His sacking, with Hibs a full nine points clear of relegation, seemed a bit harsh. Aged just 36, he was gone exactly three years to the day (20 February) since joining the club. It could hardly be said that he had taken the club on a downward spiral. When he inherited the managerial reins from Alex McLeish, the club had gone seven matches without a win, and his time in charge had been severely hampered by injuries and suspensions, and he understandably felt he hadn't been given enough time to prove himself.

It was typical of the man that instead of showing bitterness at his dismissal, he had the dignity to say 'I will never forget these three wonderful years at Hibs, and today I am really sad because I love this club'. Moreover he was right in his assessment of Hibs over-reaction to their League position. 'Even if it is difficult at the moment, I am not at all worried that Hibernian will not stay in the Premier League, no problem at all.'

FRANCK SAUZÉE factfile

Born: Aubenas (Ardèche), France, 28 October 1965
Position: Midfield and Sweeper
Playing career: Sochaux, Marseille, Monaco, Marseille, Atalanta, RC Strasbourg, Montpellier, Hibernian

Hibs League career:

Season	Games	Goals
1998–99	9	2
1999–00	25	5
2000–01	33	2
2001–02	10	4
Total	77	13

International caps:
France Under-21 caps (1988 winners of UEFA Championship)
France: 39 caps, 9 goals (none with Hibs)

THE LIFE AND TIMES OF FRANCK SAUZÉE

Club	Season	Matches	Goals
Sochaux	1983–84	19	1
Sochaux	1984–85	37	8
Sochaux	1985–86	27	7
Sochaux	1986–87	37	8
Sochaux	1987–88	30	16
Marseille	1988–89	32	4
Marseille	1989–90	36	5
Monaco	1990–91	28	7
Marseille	1991–92	22	2
Marseille	1992–93	35	12
Atlanta Bergamo	1993–94	16	1
RC Strasbourg	1994–95	30	6
RC Strasbourg	1995–96	27	4
Montpellier	1996–97	27	7
Montpellier	1997–98	12	0
Hibernian	1998–99	9	2
Hibernian	1999–2000	25	5
Hibernian	2000–01	33	2
Hibernian	2001–02	10	4

Franck Sauzée (right) with teammate Alex Marinkov.

GARRY O'CONNOR

In the modern era Garry O'Connor was a hero to thousands of young Hibernian supporters. Tall and muscular, he brought a directness and verve to the traditionally highly-visible role of centre-forward. In moving to Russian football in 2006, he made a ground-breaking transfer and one that captured the imagination of the British footballing public.

A no-nonsense, fairly uncomplicated striker, he developed significantly as a player at Hibs. When he first broke into the team his raw power and sheer spontaneity made him a huge hit. Playing alongside the likes of Franck Sauzée and Russell Latapy, he began to mature into a fine forward. He was capped by Scotland at full international level before even making an Under-21 outing, and by the time he was contemplating life in Moscow he was an accomplished player who led the line with some authority.

Garry Lawrence O'Connor was signed from Salveson Boys Club in May 1999. But while this had been a fruitful recruiting ground for Hibernian, for a number of years it was equally a virtual Hibs Boys Club, where youngsters of promise were 'farmed out' before stepping up to the club. The close links forged between the two organisations ensured that Hibs could feed their promising youngsters there and monitor their development.

In O'Connor's case the opportunity to join Hibs was perfect. He had been a Hibees supporter from boyhood and watched the club from the terraces in the early 90s. When I spoke to him, shortly after he had broken into the first team, this connection was very much in his mind.

'I always followed the Hibs. It's a real achievement for me to play here. I can remember as a wee boy watching the likes of Darren Jackson and Kevin Harper and being mesmerised and wanting to follow in their footsteps. Lots of my pals still come to Easter Road every week, and they will enjoy giving me a hard time when I venture near the East Stand [the traditional stomping ground of the hard core Hibees].'

A glut of goals in the Under-18 and Under-21 sides soon saw his name rise up the ranks (he had five in one Under-21 match against Dundee). Another bonus for O'Connor was the chance to team up with young fellow-striker Derek Riordan. The two had known each other from primary school days and forged an uncanny link on the field that would serve Hibs well. As Riordan once noted to me:

'We played together at Granton (in Edinburgh) as Under-11s and 12s and really got on well. We both played up front, and we had a brilliant understanding of each other's games. Garry went to Salveson, and I moved on to Hutcheson Vale (and usually got the upperhand in games between us), but when we both came to Hibs we reformed our partnership and seemed to click right away. I loved playing alongside Garry, and I think we had the same mind-set about the game and knew instinctively where each other would be.'

Alex McLeish, the highly-likable Hibernian boss, had a system in operation that loaned young players out to lower League clubs. This gave the youngsters a taste of the commitment needed to succeed in the game, regular first-team football and a look at life away from a big club. It was a system that worked well for Kenny Miller at Stenhousemuir, Ian Murray at Alloa and Tom McManus at Airdrie.

Peterhead were the beneficiaries of O'Connor's latent talents in 2000–01. The north-east club were celebrating their first season in the Scottish League and called upon the young player in the early part of the campaign. He responded by netting once in his four League games, and that against local rivals Elgin City.

Finally, in April 2001 he made his Hibernian first-team debut as a substitute at Dundee. Hibs won 2–0 thanks to goals by the French duo of Marc Libbra and David Zitelli, and O'Connor was clearly unperturbed by

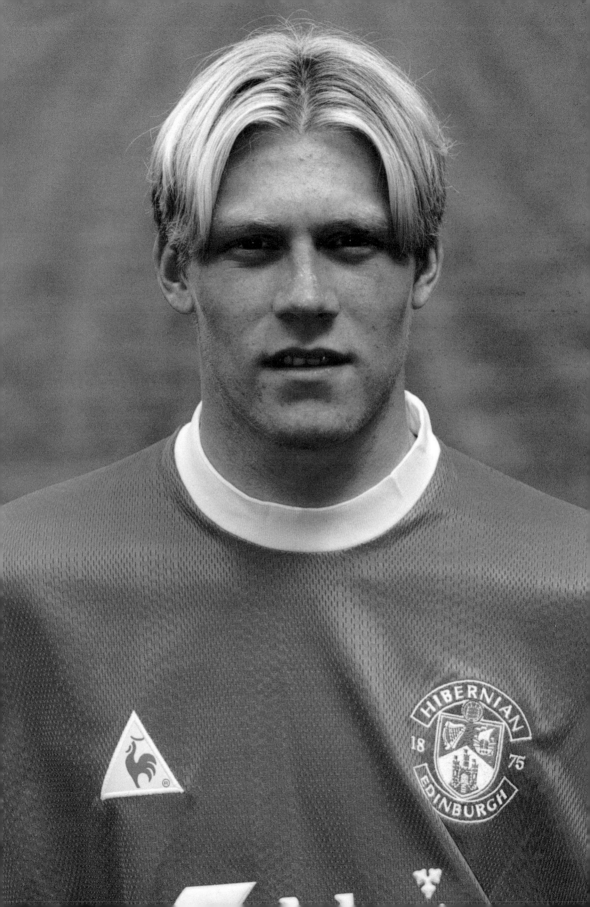

appearing on the same pitch as legendary Argentinean striker Claudio Caniggia. Along with Tom McManus and Mark Dempsie, his arrival was a sure sign that the work of youth co-ordinator John Park was reaping rewards away from the glare of first-team activity.

In the summer of 2001 Alex McLeish took O'Connor on the club's summer tour to France, and the youngster responded by scoring against Olympique Marseille and Concarneau. Within the week he was asked to lead the line for Hibs in a friendly at the slightly less salubrious Gala Fairydean. If his goals in France had caused a little comment then his four-goal salvo in the Scottish Borders really caught the eye. Why had O'Connor taken the scene by storm? Well, in his own brief words, he captured the essence of what he could bring to a fairly cosmopolitan side: 'I'm a big, confident boy'.

In only the second League game of the season an innocuous looking challenge resulted in O'Connor breaking a metatarsal bone in his foot. Thus, the youngster's promising career was halted in its tracks, and supporters would have to wait to see if they had a worthy successor to the mantle worn in the past by striking successes such as Reilly, Baker, Stein and Miller.

But for O'Connor the biggest influence on his steady progress and the best aid to his mental as well as physical recovery was Donald Park. The former Hearts and Partick Thistle midfielder nurtured and steered many young Hibs players through the system.

'When I broke my foot up at Dens Park so early in what was going to be my big breakthrough season, I don't mind admitting I was gutted. Donald Park was great at that stage and re-assured me that I would bounce back. He also encouraged me to really stick in when I got back because with people like Paco Luna and Craig Brewster on the scene I couldn't afford to relax against the competition. Equally important in a situation like that was our fitness coach Dougie Fowler, who plotted my recuperation programme.'

O'Connor was back in the first team by December and firing in shots from all angles. His vigour was the perfect antidote to a season that had seen Alex McLeish depart for Rangers and Franck Sauzée step into the manager's chair. Where Paco Luna, Craig Brewster and David Zitelli relied on guile and craft, the young Edinburgh lad went for route one: peppering the opposition goal with shots at every opportunity. His first goal at senior level came against Celtic at Easter Road and owed much to the confidence of youth. Before a live SKY television audience he latched onto a poor John Hartson clearance and with unwavering alacrity drove the loose ball swiftly beyond Rab Douglas.

Too young to be seriously affected by the floundering reign of Franck Sauzée, O'Connor knuckled down to the task in hand, and as the season neared its end he scored in five consecutive League games (against St Johnstone, Livingston, Hearts and in two games against Dundee United). He was the first Hibs player to complete that feat since the 1980s, when Gordon Rae had a similar purple patch in the 1981–82 campaign.

That run of goals was crucial to Hibs. When Alex McLeish had left to become Rangers manager the club were not playing well and things went from bad to worse under Franck Sauzée as a crisis of confidence affected a club that only months before had contested a Scottish Cup Final. When Sauzée was removed after 69 short days, the task of resurrecting the club fell to Bobby Williamson, and there is little doubt that the input of youngsters like Ian Murray and Garry O'Connor was central to Hibs pulling away from relegation.

O'Connor was the SPL Player of the Month for March 2002, having never received the Young Player of the Year award. Indeed there was some irony that he was actually younger than the player receiving the Young Player of the Month award!

Then, astonishingly, O'Connor compounded that achievement by being capped at full international level in April without ever having played at a lesser rank.

It was the much-maligned Bertie Vogts who capped O'Connor at the tender age of 18. In stepping into the fray, he became only the fifth Scot to

be capped at that age since 1900, and he joined such notable luminaries as Denis Law and Willie Henderson. Vogts, though, had no hesitation, noting:

'O'Connor's main quality is that he's a goal getter. He's young, he's quick in the penalty box and he's aggressive. All coaches the world over like aggressive strikers.'

The match in question was a friendly against Nigeria at Pittodrie Stadium, home of Aberdeen, and in coming on as a 74th-minute substitute O'Connor put the seal on what was a season of genuine progress and promise. Vogts was certainly impressed and took the youngster to the Far East with his new-look Scotland squad.

'Playing in Hong Kong during the summer months for Scotland was a great experience for me. I had been to the likes of Finland and France with Hibs, but Asia was a different experience all together. The thing that struck me was the heat, and even though we played our games in the evening it was still very hot and humid. It taught me that there were other factors in the game beyond honing your skills and mental approach.'

At that stage his career seemed on an unbreakable upward swing, and then came the hazard that from time to time suspiciously befalls non-Old Firm youngsters. On the eve of a key clash with Rangers, stories in the press suggested that O'Connor was on the verge of moving to Ibrox.

The more cynical among the Hibernian support would question the intentions of such stories and perhaps suggest that the timing indicated that a little malice was in hand. Others would say the story breaking at that point was just unfortunate timing. Whatever the reasoning, the outcome was that O'Connor's career stuttered horribly when he answered quite honestly and openly that he would view going to Rangers as a career progression.

Worse still, when the transfer speculation subsided with no move having taken place, the youngster was caught in no-mans land. It took the

Hibernian support considerable time to 'forgive and forget' and for an awkward month or two he was booed by a section of the Easter Road faithful.

It was to his eternal credit that he knuckled down to the task in hand and began to resurrect his Hibernian career. Much of the support he got came from Bobby Williamson.

'The gaffer was a really big help to me. He stood by me when things were not going too well, and I was delighted to be repaying him with a few goals. I have to say I was also pleased to be scoring for the fans again, I fully understood that they were desperately disappointed that I had said I would welcome the chance to play for a huge club like Rangers. Fortunately, most of them understood what the opportunity offered me on a personal level and they stood by me, and it gave me a real kick to repay them for their support. Remember I was able to stay with Hibs for a quite while after the transfer speculation ended'.

Hibernian Under-18s in 2001. O'Connor is on the back row, third from left. His great friend and fellow striker Derek Riordan is on the front row, second from the left. They both progressed to the Scotland side, as did Steven Whittaker, who is to the immediate right of the two goalkeepers in the centre row.

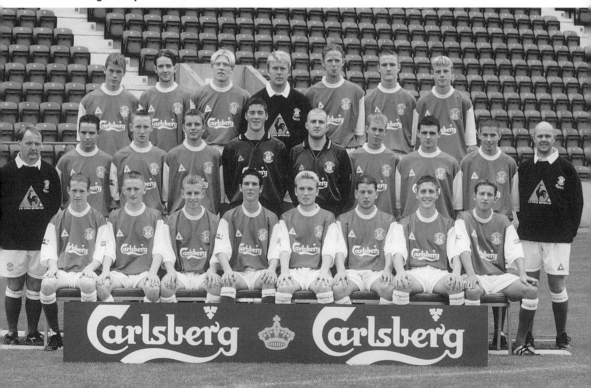

2002–03 saw O'Connor back among the goals, and in October of that season he scored two that will live in the Hibs memory banks for some time. The game was played at Partick and saw Hibs power home 3–0. Just before half-time he thundered an unstoppable drive into the roof of the Partick Thistle net from just inside their half. Then in the second half he upstaged that wonder strike when knocking the ball over Stephen Craigan's head and volleying home the dropping ball. It was a master class in finishing and showed that he had put the Rangers on-off transfer saga behind him.

For many strikers one or two goals can define their career, and while O'Connor's strikes against Partick Thistle clearly impressed they paled into insignificance on 17 August 2003. As a new season got underway, Hibs found themselves starting their home League campaign with a match against Hearts. With both sides having won their opening League fixture, a tumultuous atmosphere welcomed the sides. In a truly pulsating derby, Hibs found themselves 'up against it' when Grant Brebner was sent off in the first half.

O'Connor, who hadn't played in the first match, was introduced as a second-half substitute and gave his usual hard-running, powerful display. Then in the final minute a long ball sent him clean through on goal and a composed low finish sent three-quarters of Easter Road into raptures. Moilanen, in the Hearts goal, had little chance. It was a derby winner of classic proportions, and for O'Connor it ensured he would start every match until injured in February.

Club captain Ian Murray was among those who were torn between being happier for O'Connor or for the club:

'Hearts probably expected to win when Grant was sent off. It was great to score so late on, and personally I was delighted that it was Garry who scored such an important goal. Big Garry had to battle his way back after a sticky patch. I think every single Hibs player knew he had a chance when he got the ball in that position because he hits the ball so well. He really took the chance and hit it so hard and low that Moilanen didn't really have a hope of saving it. The other big plus was that Garry scored so late; it was perfect timing as Hearts had no time to come back.'

Hibs' last-minute derby win marred by referee drama

Police are forced to thwart fan's attempt to confront Dougal

HIBERNIAN	1
HEARTS	0

Scorer: O'Connor 1901

ROB ROBERTSON
AT EASTER ROAD

PASSION inflames each and every Edinburgh derby but yesterday at Easter Road such emotions spilled over in sad, dramatic scenes which marred an unexpected victory from 10-man Hibs.

It was a Sunday afternoon of extremes which ranged from the worst refereeing display for many years from Stuart Dougal to a sublime last-minute winner from substitute Garry O'Connor.

Events over the weekend have also reopened the debate over whether the time is right for barriers to be erected to keep supporters off the pitch.

On Saturday at Pittodrie, an Aberdeen supporter ran 40 yards to try to attack Fernando Ricksen of Rangers. Yesterday at Easter Road a fan, believed to be a carer for a disabled supporter who was trackside, ran on at half-time to try to confront Stuart Dougal and only the swift action of Hearts goalkeeper Tepi Moilanen stopped a major incident.

At the final whistle, two minutes after O'Connor's winning goal, hundreds of Hibs supporters invaded the park to taunt the Hearts fans in the south stand. They responded by throwing plastic bottles and other objects.

Afterwards, the animosity spilled out on to the streets with confrontation between both sets of supporters breaking out after a gate keeping them apart outside the main stand was kicked open. Police struggled to shut the gate and regain order and it was only when mounted officers arrived that the situation calmed down.

David Forsyth, the Hibs spokesman, said that they would be liaising with Lothian and Borders police and appropriate action would be taken against supporters who had been on the pitch.

With all the madness going on it was easy to forget that there was a game of football going on. In a way, the last-minute O'Connor goal switched the headlines away from Dougal, who still has to be taken to task for the way he spoiled the game. By full time he had handed out seven bookings for reasons best known to himself and dished out an unjustified red card to Grant Brebner.

He also managed to miss a challenge from Andy Webster on Scott Brown when the Scotland internationalist raised his fist to the youngster and was lucky to escape with just a booking.

Once Brebner was sent off in 37 minutes for a mistimed tackle on Robert Sloan you expected Hearts to go on and win the game. However, as Craig Levein, the Hearts coach, said afterwards: "We maybe had more chances but they had more will and desire to keep going than us.

"We had a chance to equalise at the very end through Steven Pressley but if that had gone in it would have simply papered over the cracks in our performance. We can have no complaints."

From a Hibs perspective it was an unlikely win which had been a long time coming. It has taken Bobby Williamson six attempts to beat Hearts and that, plus the fact the Tynecastle side stole a last minute win through Phil Stamp in the same fixture last season, made the success all the more sweet for the long-suffering Easter Road supporters.

Williamson chose his words carefully at the end regarding the Brebner sending-off and the performance of the referee, his comments clearly lightened by the win.

"The referee will work out whether he had a decent game or not," said Williamson. "I did not see it as a straight red card as I felt the player cut across him and Grant felt the same."

It usually takes a lot to get a smile on the face of Williamson but with two league wins on the bounce he will be thinking he has at last turned the corner with a team who have under-performed since his arrival.

Ian Murray, the Hibs captain, was one of the inspirations behind the win but his overexuberant celebrations in front of the Hearts support at the end did himself little favours.

"I felt the sending-off of Grant was a poor decision but it brought the best out of us,"

said Murray. "I saw a few fans on the park at the end but it happened during the 4-4 game when Hearts fans were jubilant on their own patch. It was to be expected."

Murray may be guilty of naivety making such comments but there was no denying the incredible atmosphere which gripped Easter Road yesterday. Despite Dougal trying to strangle the encounter, it was still a decent contest with Hibs hitting a post through Jarkko Wiss and Yannick Zambernardi missing with an easy header.

Hearts looked much stronger in midfield throughout with Stamp, Scott Severin, and Paul Hartley running the show. However movement up front was poor with Mark de Vries looking unfit and Dennis Wyness still struggling to cope with the pace of the SPL to such an extent that Levein will be getting concerned about his below-par performances.

In the end the day belonged to Hibs and although the pitch invasion and the attempted attack on the referee marred proceedings the character they showed was second to none.

What made the victory even more unlikely was the fact that despite Williamson making five summer signings none of them started yesterday and he relied on last year's under-achievers to bring him his most savoured victory as the Hibs manager.

It has been a long time coming but in the end the dramatic events could lead to a bit of sunshine of Leith after a long, bleak period of drizzle.

Hibernian (4-4-2) Andersson, Orman, Doumbe, Smith, Zambernardi, McManus, (Caldwell, 81), Brebner, Wiss (Glass 89), Murray, Scott Brown, Riordan (O'Connor 68). Subs: Hodgsson, Whittaker. **Sent Off** Brebner (37). **Booked** Doumbe, Orman, McManus, O'Connor.

Hearts (4-4-2) Moilanen, Maybury, Pressley, Webster, McGrenn, Hartley, Severin, Stamp (Sloan 88) yende 45, de Vries (McKenna 68), Wyness (Pirrs 78). Subs: Gordon, MacFarlane. **Booked** Severin, Webster, Boruc.

Referee S Dougal

WORRYING TIMES: Police restrain an irate Hibs fan as he attempts to approach referee Stuart Dougal at half-time

MAKING A FIST OF IT: Ian Murray, the Hibs captain, celebrates with his team-mates after scoring the winning goal in time added on at Easter Road yesterday. Pictures: Jim Galloway

Making the headlines: Ian Murray celebrates O'Connor's 90th-minute derby winner.

The goal gave the Lothians and Borders police plenty to think about. O'Connor's goal sparked wild celebrations among the Hibs support, who staged a mini pitch invasion, but infuriated the Hearts followers, some of whom vented their spleen in the streets surrounding the stadium. Passions had clearly been running high, and, in winning with 10 men and ending a 22-month period without a derby win, Hibs fans had overdone the celebrations. Also an attempted attack on the referee at half-time by a fan reportedly watching over a disabled friend added to the mayhem.

The national press were quick to recognise that after a calamitous run of conceding late goals, particularly in the derby fixture, Hibs had earned their break. *The Scotsman* summed it up quite neatly.

'It had to happen. If and when Hibs were going to win an Edinburgh derby, they were surely fated to do so with a late goal. And so it turned out yesterday as Garry O'Connor's winner came a minute into time added on.'

Nevertheless, the season was tainted with disappointment. By March 2004 Hibs had battled through to the CIS League Cup Final. O'Connor had played his part in grabbing two goals in a first-round 9–0 demolition of Montrose and led the line with vigour in a 2–1 quarter-final triumph over Celtic.

In the semi-finals Hibs overcame a lacklustre Rangers in a match decided on penalty kicks. The tie ended up 1–1, but Hibs dominated the latter stage of the game and were unfortunate to be taken to extra-time and then the dreaded shoot-out. O'Connor missed one of the spot-kicks and like most Edinburgh fans was grateful for Daniel Andersson's three saves and Colin Murdock's decisive penalty conversion. And thus to the Final against Livingston. The bookies thought Hibs would win, the press thought Hibs would triumph, and so did a 37,000-strong travelling army of Hibs fans. But in a dreadful anti-climax Hibs gave a woeful showing at Hampden and slumped to a 0–2 defeat. O'Connor so nearly scored the opening goal when he latched onto a rebound from Roddy McKenzie but saw his effort hacked to safety on the line by Marvin Andrews. It was as near as Hibs came to snatching something from a bitterly disappointing match. Once again Hibernian had come up lacking in a big Hampden occasion.

By the 2004–05 season the purposeful O'Connor was the leading light in Scotland's Under-21 side. He scored at Perth against Moldova and had a notable encounter against Spain in a friendly. By March 2005 his rehabilitation was complete when he came off the bench for Scotland's full side in a World Cup qualifier against the mighty Italy in Milan.

At domestic level his boyhood partnership with Derek Riordan was reaping real rewards for Hibs. Under Tony Mowbray's shrewd and youthful guidance Riordan won the Young Player of the Month award four times, and he was quick to place some of the thanks at O'Connor's door. While Riordan had 20 League goals, O'Connor's haul of 14 was impressive. The

Hibs delight as youngsters keep nerve in shootout drama to claim final berth

Another trophy slips from grasp of McLeish's Rangers

HIBERNIAN	**1**
RANGERS	**1**

Aet Hibs win 4-3 on penalties.
Scorers: Hibernian – Dobbie (79); Rangers – Mols (40).

GRAHAM SPIERS
AT HAMPDEN PARK

THERE can be no dispute about it. Hibs walked out of Hampden last night, their chests rightly puffed and the club's reputation given a fresh sheen, after a thrilling CIS Insurance Cup semi-final which raged for 120 minutes before lapsing into the drama of penalties.

Over the piece it was a deserved Hibs win, for the sheer guts and the array of skill with which they turned this match on its head.

The penalty shoot-out became gripping. Of the first five penalties struck, only one, converted by Gary Caldwell, made it into the net. Daniel Andersson and Stefan Klos produced a sequence of marvellous saves, Klos in particular from Garry O'Connor — perhaps the finest Hampden has witnessed in a long time.

At 1-1 after 90 minutes, Hibs finally ran out 4-3 winners when Frank de Boer revisited his Euro 2000 spot-kick nightmare, striking the base of a post when he was required to score and keep Rangers alive.

It was a sweet night for Bobby Williamson, this colourful, impressive, hard-working manager, whose sojourn at Hibs for two years has so often resembled a reprise of the life of Job. Williamson does a lot of bawling and isn't averse to the odd catfight, but no neutral at Hampden last night begrudged him this moment.

It will be the first time since ...rs won the Scottish Cup in

Alex McLeish, a man who in his own way, like Williamson, is not having an easy season. Rangers are trailing 11 points behind Celtic in the league and the two remaining cups had been seen as essential to Rangers' self-respect. Technically, with the league title still in the offing, this is the first trophy McLeish has contested and failed to land for Rangers.

Hibs' young side were a thrilling credit to their manager. Rangers had studiously shackled them for a good hour before players like Derek Riordan, Kevin Thomson, Stephen Dobbie, and O'Connor suddenly blew the game into life.

As the affair was turned on its head, and Rangers suddenly came under a welter of Hibs

The Dutchman was lucky to get away with that assault but Hibs would have their reward. Hibs' equaliser after 78 minutes, levelling Michael Mols' first-half opener, was a thrilling moment for a team of nice touches which had none the less failed to cause Rangers much anxiety. Dobbie, the former Ibrox youngster who had been on the park for only three minutes, took Thomson's quick pass and smashed his shot past Klos from 12 yards. It was just reward for the dramatic final 25 minutes Hibs contributed to this game.

The match came in mesmerising spurts. Andersson's fine save from Mikel Arteta's first-half penalty was such a mo... n. On top of Ricksen's

It has been said before ... it is like a near-death experience watching Ross trying to play football. Rangers' poor full back, a jittery performer low on confidence, receives regular pannings from the touchline from McLeish, and this match was no different. Some people have seen high-rises in Kazakhstan that are safer than Ross prowling with a football.

Don't say the game is short on miracles. In the 40th minute, having struck a stray pass here and a botched pass there, Ross embarked on a brave, imaginative run before releasing Mols in the heart of the Hibs area. Mols didn't stop to count his luck before lashing his shot past Andersson from 10 yards.

The game had plodded along

Ross, Ricksen, and Mols which, slicing through Hibs, released Ronald de Boer into Andersson's area. The goalkeeper's subsequent dive at de Boer's ankles took the feet from under the Dutchman, but Andersson quickly atoned, plunging to his left to block Arteta's unconvincing penalty.

It was a wearying vigil waiting for Hibs to create some chances. Klos was required only to fist away a couple of crosses, yet, even when apparently redundant, he would in a flash be sprinting from his box to clear from behind Craig Moore and Frank de Boer.

The way this match was suddenly stopped in its tracks, and then reversed in Hibs' favour, was astonishing. It took 14 penalties, and seven misses, before Hibs finally ensured their return to Hampden.

Hibernian (4-4-2) Andersson; Caldwell, Murdock, Doumbe, Edge; Dobbie 79), S Brown, Whittaker (Fletcher 97), Reid (McManus 65); Thomson, O'Connor. Rangers (4-4-2) Klos; Ross (Nimni 49), F de Boer, Moore, Ball; Ricksen, Arteta (Khizanishvili 73), Namouchi, de Boer (Ostenstad 73); Mols, Subir Capucho; McGregor. Booked Andersson; Vanoli. Referee Kenny Clark (Rutherglen).

Reaction, Page 35

Reaction, Page 35

JOY UNCONFINED: The Hibs players react to the realisation that they are through to the final of the CIS Insurance Cup following Frank de Boer's sudden-death penalty miss. Picture: Jeff J Mitchell/Reuters

TOMORROW

EXCLUSIVE INTERVIEW NEIL LENNON

Despite having his penalty saved by Rangers' Stefan Klos, Garry O'Connor and Hibs came out victors of this semi-final at Hampden Park.

only disappointment for him was seeing Riordan net in six consecutive League games, thus virtually erasing his five-match sequence of 2002 from the record books.

But amid all this success the undeniable truth was that neither O'Connor nor Riordan had picked up any silverware at Easter Road. The 2004–05 season was a point in case. A third-place finish in the League behind the wealthy Glasgow duo of Rangers and Celtic was clearly a notable achievement, but, in losing a Scottish Cup semi-final and a League Cup quarter-final to a very ordinary Dundee United, they revealed their Achilles heel: Hibs were unable to consistently 'put away' lesser sides.

Thus, O'Connor could hardly refuse a proposed move to Lokomotiv Moscow that surfaced in early 2006. The Russian Premier League club offered to take his wages from £2,000 per week to £16,000. This was a financial boost that promised to make him a multi-millionaire. As the Hibs manager at the time Tony Mowbray said:

'It's a life-changing money opportunity for Garry. Obviously as a football manager I'm unhappy to lose any of my best players, but an overriding factor for me is that this is not just a small increase in the player's salary, but a massive one. You can't deny a player that, and the human side has to come into it. We work to a budget at Easter Road, and the wages Lokomotiv offered Garry would catapult him out of our stratosphere.'

For the Hibernian hierarchy the move was a sweet reward in a period that had seen them lose Ian Murray for nothing (to Rangers) and Gary Caldwell to Celtic in similar circumstances.

Another factor influencing Tony Mowbray's relaxed attitude was the fact that a much needed training facility seemed to be a likely outcome of Hibs receiving a £1.6m fee. Mowbray had long cited the lack of quality training facilities as a bar to Hibs jumping 'to the next level'. The directors for their part also had the redevelopment of the old East Stand in their sights.

The move came in March 2006, when the Russian football season was enjoying its winter break and preparing for a new campaign. Lokomotiv, who were Russian champions in 2004, were desperate to regain their title and struggling to compete with city rivals Spartak and CSKA. Having identified a lack of goals as a key deficiency, they targeted 22-year-old O'Connor as the solution to their problems.

By this stage Scottish football was accustomed to eastern European footballers earning their living here. Indeed, over the city, at Hearts, the flying winger Deividas Cesnauskis encouraged O'Connor to take the plunge. He pointed out that Lokomotiv lacked nothing in ambition, having built a new stadium and a superb training complex. Cesnauskis certainly knew the lie of the land, having played with both Dinamo and Lokomotiv in Russia's capital and won a Championship medal with the latter.

'What Garry might find hard are the distances involved when travelling to games. Here in Scotland you can drive to any ground, but in Russia away matches involve taking flights. I suppose the other big change will be the lifestyle as no Russian city is quite like Scotland.'

O'Connor had been lined up to face Scotland against Switzerland in a Hampden friendly when news of the transfer broke, and he was hastily withdrawn from the squad in order to undergo the obligatory medical. By that stage his reputation in Scotland was solid, having gained four full international caps to accompany his eight Under-21 awards. Scotland assistant manager Tommy Burns was happy to release the young striker noting:

'It's fantastic money and a great deal for Hibs. I suppose Hibs will look at it as a young player they have spent a lot of time nurturing and developing, who is now an international player and looking to go to the next level. The team buying him are taking a player of exciting potential, whose best years are still ahead of him.

'There are some top players in Russia these days. Brazilian, Portuguese and Yugoslavian players have made the move. Garry should benefit from training and playing in that environment.'

Thus 22-year-old O'Connor departed as he neared the peak of his powers, or as Mowbray noted 'He's not the finished article, but he knows that. Any different experiences in football can make you a better player'. He had scored 14 goals in the 2005–06 season, including one in what was his final match – against Falkirk in the Scottish Cup quarter-final tie that booked Hibs a spot in the last four of the grand old competition. Hibs, seeking their first Scottish Cup triumph since 1902, were left facing a semi-final against their city-rivals Hearts without their star asset but with money in the bank.

Life changed quickly for O'Connor. First up was a testing two-day medical in Munich and then it was off to the warmer climes of Spain as

Lokomotiv trained in preparation for the start of their season. Coached by Serbian guru Slaboliub Muslin, he made his debut against Marbella of the Spanish Second Division and reflected on his ground-breaking move:

'It was a big challenge coming here, and it dragged on a bit. Over the past month I've had to do a lot of thinking, while remaining focused for Hibs. But it's all worked out well; the club's happy, my agent's happy, my family's happy, and I am chuffed to bits. It will be a great opportunity, and I'm going there determined to grab it and help them win things.'

Only time would tell if the young man who had thrilled thousands at Easter Road would be able to translate his Scottish skills to the demands of Premier League football on the other side of Europe. For Hibs, meanwhile, the Scottish Cup semi-final was lost disastrously by a thumping 0–4 in Hampden's first all-Edinburgh clash, and how Hibs could have done with O'Connor on that bleak afternoon. By one of those strange twists of fate that mark football, Hearts were led by a new coach from Lithuania, Valdas Ivanauskas... the same man who had steered Vetra Vilnius to Intertoto Cup victory over Hibs when Tony Mowbray first took over at Hibs.

GARRY O'CONNOR factfile

Born: Edinburgh, 7 May 1983
Position: Striker
Playing career: Hibernian, Lokomotiv Moscow

Hibs League career:

Season	Games	Goals
2000–01	1	0
2001–02	19	9
2002–03	24	6
2003–04	33	4
2004–05	36	14
2005–06	25	11
Total	138	44

Above total does not include 4 games (and one goal) while on loan to Peterhead in season 2000–01.

International caps:

Scotland Under-21: 8 games, 2 goals

Scotland: 4 games

O'CONNOR'S GOALS

2 February 2002: Home v Celtic

2 March 2002: Home v St Johnstone

9 March 2002: Away v Livingston

16 March 2002: Home v Hearts

23 March 2002: Away v Dundee United

7 April 2002: Away v Dundee United

21 April 2002: Home v Motherwell (2)

27 April 2002: Away v St Johnstone

18 August 2002: Home v Rangers

24 August 2002: Away v Dundee

24 September 2002: Away v Alloa (LC)

5 October 2002: Home v Dundee United

19 October 2002: Away v Partick Thistle (2)

24 October 2002: Home v Rangers (LC)

8 February 2003: Away v Motherwell

17 August 2003: Home v Hearts

23 September 2003: Home v Montrose (2) (LC)

3 January 2004: Home v Partick

24 January 2004: Away v Kilmarnock

8 May 2004: Away v Aberdeen

14 August 2004: Home v Motherwell (2)

28 August 2004: Home v Dundee (2)

22 September 2004: Away v Albion Rovers (LC)

2 October 2004: Away v Dunfermline

16 October 2004: Home v Dundee United

27 December 2004: Away v Dundee United

15 January 2005: Away v Livingston

5 February 2005: Home v Brechin City (2) (SC)

19 February 2005: Home v Dundee (2)

26 February 2005: Home v St Mirren (SC)

2 April 2005: Home v Dundee United

13 April 2005: Home v Hearts

30 April 2005: Away v Celtic

30 July 2005: Home v Dunfermline

13 August 2005: Home v Livingston

10 September 2005: Home v Dundee United

26 October 2005: Away v Dunfermline (2)

29 October 2005: Home v Hearts

5 November 2005: Away v Livingston

27 November 2005: Home v Rangers

2 January 2006: Away v Kilmarnock

7 January 2006: Home v Arbroath (SC)

28 January 2006: Away v Hearts

4 February 2006: Away v Rangers (SC)

8 February 2006: Home v Livingston

25 February 2006: Away v Falkirk (SC)